Navigating the New Pedagogy

Six Principles That Transform Teaching

Jeff Halstead

ROWMAN & LITTLEFIELD EDUCATION

A division of
ROWMAN & LITTLEFIELD PUBLISHERS, INC.
Lanham • New York • Toronto • Plymouth, UK

Published by Rowman & Littlefield Education
A division of Rowman & Littlefield Publishers, Inc.
A wholly owned subsidary of The Rowman & Littlefield Publishing Group, Inc.
4501 Forbes Boulevard, Suite 200, Lanham, Maryland 20706
http://www.rowmaneducation.com

Estover Road, Plymouth PL6 7PY, United Kingdom

British Library Cataloguing in Publication Information Available

Library of Congress Cataloging-in-Publication Data

Halstead, Jeff, 1958–
    Navigating the new pedagogy : six principles that transform teaching / Jeff
Halstead.
        p. cm.
    Summary: "Navigating the New Pedagogy Six Principles that Transform
is written to give teachers a vision of current, best 21st century classroom
practice. Teachers, administrators, and education professors will find ideas
that will help transform classrooms into positive, productive learning
environments"—Provided by publisher.
    Includes bibliographical references and index.
    ISBN 978-1-61048-023-9 (hardback) — ISBN 978-1-61048-024-6 (paper)
— ISBN 978-1-61048-025-3 (ebook)
    1. Effective teaching—United States. 2. Teacher effectiveness—United
States. 3. Teacher-student relationships—United States. 4. Lesson planning—
United States. I. Title.
    LB1025.3.H355 2011
    371.102—dc22   2011001040

♾™ The paper used in this publication meets the minimum requirements of
American National Standard for Information Sciences—Permanence of Paper
for Printed Library Materials, ANSI/NISO Z39.48-1992.

Printed in the United States of America

To Deb, loving wife, nurturing mom, and master teacher, without whose guidance and support this book would not have been possible.

In all our efforts for education—in providing adequate research and study—we must never lose sight of the very heart of education: good teaching itself. Good teachers do not just happen, they are the product of the highest of personal motivation.

—Dwight D. Eisenhower

Contents

The Classroom as the Pivotal Point for True Reform

Fenwick W. English,
R. Wendell Eaves Senior Distinguished Professor
of Educational Leadership
School of Education, University of North Carolina at Chapel Hill

In his best-selling book *The Predictable Failure of Educational Reform: Can We Change Course Before It's Too Late?* the late Seymour Sarason chastised policy wonks and other so-called educational-reform experts for overlooking the most important feature of making reform really work: *the classroom teacher.* Sarason said the lack of teacher involvement in reform "comes close to being universal in school systems. That omission in part explains why reform efforts fail as they do, why teachers regard administrators as people who have forgotten what it is like to be teachers."[1]

Jeff Halstead has taken up Sarason's mantra in this insightful book. For example, Sarason began his critique of traditional educational reform by indicating that certain "unquestioned bedrock assumptions" had to be faced. Among them was the concept of the "encapsulated classroom and school," that is, where students were fixated in rows facing the teacher, who dispensed knowledge as though the pupils were empty vessels. This "pouring in knowledge" had to be replaced by a more social-cognitive theory of learning for any reform to succeed. Classroom teachers had to be energized and some "unlearning" had to occur. By this, Sarason explained that "unlearning old attitudes, acquiring new ones, accepting new responsibilities, trying the new and risking failure, unrealistic time perspectives and expectations, limited resources, struggles as a consequence of altered power relationships" were the heart of any true reform.[2] Sarason was trenchantly insightful when he warned, "One can change curricula, standards, and a lot of other things by legislation and fiat, but if the regularities of the classroom remain unexamined and unchanged, the failure of the reforms is guaranteed."[3]

All one has to do today is to review the many schemes and recommendations for how business, government, politicians, and editorial-page pundits will improve education to see how they all miss what Sarason identified as the pivotal point for true reform. This is where Jeff Halstead's book is so critical. Halstead, who has trained hundreds of teachers in becoming more than lecturers and pitchers of knowledge, delves into the actual strategies, tactics, and techniques of dramatically changing the ethos of the "encapsulated classroom." He shows how to do it and then gives example after example of its salutary impact on teaching practice. It is rare indeed to find someone with his insights and experience in the real world of teaching. This is where the solution to the achievement gap really lies: not in the merit-pay schemes, union-busting tactics, firing the principal, removing the school board, abolishing schools of education and closing down schools serving the poor run by those who have not a clue of what goes on in classrooms, and unlocking the keys to improved student learning. I think Halstead's book exposes, as so much corporate claptrap, the notion that an educational leader doesn't really have to know anything about teaching to be successful.[4]

So, I invite the reader to enter Jeff Halstead's real classroom-teaching world and discover not only the joys of teaching, but the excitement of learning. For a true educator, that's all that is really needed to keep one going, and it's where real educational reform begins and ends.

NOTES

1. Seymour Sarason, *The Predictable Failure of Educational Reform: Can We Change Course Before It's Too Late?* (San Francisco, CA: Jossey-Bass, 1990), 166.

2. Sarason, *Predictable Failure*, 146.

3. Sarason, *Predictable Failure*, 70.

4. Thomas B. Fordham Institute and Broad Foundation, "Better Leaders for America's Schools: A Manifesto," 2003, at broadeducation.org/asset/1128 -betterleadersforamericasschools.pdf (accessed Dec. 19, 2010).

Preface

Over the past decade, I have had the good fortune to be immersed in unbelievably rich opportunities to train educators in the newest cutting-edge professional-development philosophies. I became a leader, presenter, and curriculum designer for the Teacher Leadership Project, which intensively trained more than 3,500 teachers to infuse technology into "understanding by design"-based, constructivist teaching— one of the most successful professional-development initiatives ever conducted in Washington state.

From there, I completed my National Board certification and have spent years facilitating cohorts through this rigorous process. For six years, I developed and led professional development for Spokane public schools, which taught hundreds of teachers to create learning environments rich in the current, most effective teaching practices and technology. As a result, I spent countless days in classrooms observing highly adept teachers, assisting lessons, and seeing firsthand what really improves learning. My educational background also includes more than 20 years of teaching secondary students, so I know the challenges educators face.

These experiences working with a broad base of current educational initiatives and the constant investigation into what works best form the basis for this book.

ACKNOWLEDGMENTS

Thanks to Beth McGibbon, Eric Magi, Patrick Daisley, and Susie Gerard for your comments, suggestions, and contributions. To my sons,

John and Joey—thank you for your constant love and support. Many thanks to my wife, Deb, for our wonderful family, home, and memories and believing in me for the last 22 years. And to my editor, Tom Koerner—thank you for your faith and belief in the importance of this book.

Introduction

Perhaps it is human nature to search for the quick or magical fix. While watching the television or scanning the pages of newspapers or magazines, readers and viewers are confronted with products that promise to change their lives dramatically. Longtime veterans in the field of education have sat through innumerable workshops and training sessions where the presenters made similar claims. Whether it be Instructional Theory into Practice, GESA (Gender Expectation and Student Achievement), or Cooperative Learning (recycled fifteen years later as student collaboration) of decades ago, or Understanding by Design, Differentiated Instruction, Classroom Assessment for Student Learning, and Standards-Based Grading of today, these educational practices promise to bring a dramatic rise in student engagement and achievement.

Unlike many television or print ads, each of the major professional-development initiatives listed above has made a positive impact on student learning. In the last decade, the education profession has been undergoing a tremendous transformation in philosophy and pedagogy, largely because of these new ideas.

As a result, a new vision for classroom practice has emerged that looks very different from the teaching that existed previously. This 21st-century teaching is a *synthesis* of effective curriculum, big ideas, nurturing relationships, appropriate assessment, articulated standards, technology, and solid understanding of the content being taught. It requires proficiency in a variety of skills, all of which are required for healthy, successful learning environments for students.

Like peaks rising above the clouds, six core principles emerge from the new educational theory and have the power to define and organize this new vision for classroom practice. These six principles, the topic of this book, have the power to transform teaching practice. They are based on today's best ideas and will guide teachers and administrators as they navigate the underbrush of daily practice, where critical decisions impact student lives.

Navigating the New Pedagogy: Six Principles That Transform Teaching is dedicated to the better understanding of key concepts at the heart of current, effective instructional practices. While reading, please reflect upon these principles and ways to implement them in classroom practice.

Make Kids Think

The mind is not a vessel to be filled but a fire to be kindled.

—Plutarch

Enter Patrick Daisley's high school physics classroom during the study of acceleration, and you are greeted with the clank of brass and the whirl of small cars gliding down a metal track. At each student workstation, a string runs from the small car to brass weights hanging off the edge of a table. When the car is released, the weight on the string pulls the car down a track. As the car nears the end of the track, it passes through a photo gate sensor, and a computer records the car's velocity.

Amid the classroom cacophony of clanks and crashes, students are gradually adding more weights with each test, and the computer records the greater acceleration that results. Students huddle around their hardware, release the cars, then quickly shift to view the computer screen, eager for results.

Balding, brilliant physics teacher Daisley moves among his students, answering questions and watching their processes to assure they yield accurate results. Rather than being a "sage on the stage," lecturing to his students about the forces at work in the universe, Daisley is a coach to these young adults as they use the precision of technology to gather understanding. Instead of assigning reading to open his senior physics units (starting at a *knowledge* level as other physics teachers might), Daisley creates understanding through hands-on experiments—a style of science instruction called *modeling*. He starts his units with a question or a problem to solve, but he builds student understanding carefully and intentionally.

Before he began the previous experiment, his class carefully studied the motion of objects, both constant velocity and acceleration (changes in motion). Once the students understood those concepts, they moved ahead to the study of the causes of acceleration: force, a more challenging concept. In teams, the students create a hypothesis about how this acceleration occurs; as teams, they carry out experiments using technology to test their theories.

After completing their experiments, the students analyze their graphs of acceleration that emerge, write mathematical formulas to quantify their results, and apply their learning to real-life applications. As they work, they revise their previous understanding. Rather than relying upon traditional methods of reading a concept in a textbook and committing it to memory, Daisley has found these hands-on experiments create deep conceptual understanding that endures. In fact, on a nationally known physics concept test, his high school students often outperform freshman physics majors from colleges around the country.

Take note of the cause of his success: Students use the scientific process to gain understanding. *Analysis* of their findings and *synthesis* of results—both high levels of cognition—are used to create *knowledge*.

Contrast this with the physics instructions many recall. Rather than clanking, physics classrooms were filled with the clicking of chalk as instructors drew diagrams that stretched across the room-width science blackboards. Ideas were explained in a lecture format, and experiments, when they were used, were demonstrations that supported previous instruction rather than revealed new concepts. For the most part, students were expected to absorb their understanding through textbooks, lectures, films—and not create it for themselves.

ARE STUDENTS THINKING NOW?

Classrooms should be places where great thinking occurs. Too frequently, though, they are not. If there is one major weakness of the educational system—especially at the secondary level—it is that classrooms are places where knowledge is dispensed.

Many mathematics teachers, for example, still show their students algorithms then assign thirty problems to hammer the concept home. (Students are taught to identify the Y intercept but do not know the practical application of this concept, for example.) Some English teachers use matching-answer questions to check student knowledge of characters or essay questions to assess student *recall* of past class discussions (all low-level thinking activities). History teachers lecture about the causes of the Great Depression but fail to ask students to draw parallels between the Roaring Twenties and the events leading to the Great Recession of 2008.

In the traditional classroom, students' minds are treated like grocery sacks, the purpose of each course being to add more content until the sacks are appropriately filled (content requirements), and the student is ready for checkout into the real world (graduation).

The problem with this depository form of instruction is that adult life functions contrary to it. From purchasing a new car to learning a new job, people analyze and synthesize information to create their own knowledge base. They don't purchase a manual on how to live; they learn by doing. In nearly every facet of their lives, they analyze problems, test solutions, and learn in the process. Most students recognize themselves as problem solvers in their own world. No kid takes classes on using cell phones, iPods, or computers. They figure these things out for themselves or, when confused, work with a friend to solve the problem. During the school week, though, they enter classrooms where—rather than thinking and problem solving—they are assigned textbook reading or sit through lectures or demonstrations. No wonder school bores these students.

The Reflective Teacher

- If someone were to observe my classroom, to what degree would students be deeply engaged in thinking and active learning on a day-to-day basis?

TURN BLOOM'S ON ITS HEAD

When teachers "make kids think," they design lessons where students complete activities designed to "construct meaning"—in other words, through learning activities, students *create* their own knowledge. Not only does this teaching strategy contrast with conventional teaching methods, "constructing meaning" also turns traditional implementation of Bloom's Taxonomy on its head.

When Bloom's Taxonomy was being implemented in the early 1980s (in fact, even when I was teaching a graduate-level course called "Teaching Critical Thinking Skills" in 1986), the current belief was that teachers needed to build "knowledge" and make sure students could function at the "comprehension" and "application" level first (considered lower levels of cognition) before they ever dared venture with their students into the loftier realms of "analysis," "synthesis," and "evaluation"—considered the high levels of thinking in Bloom's Taxonomy.

In other words, students first gathered knowledge through reading, lectures, media and/or explanation. Next, they were asked to explain the information (comprehension) and, if possible, apply it (application) to additional problems. In short, classrooms worked their way up the cognitive ladder (see Figure 1.1). Working at the higher levels of Bloom's was really what engaged students. Teachers just believed students *needed* to endure the painful and often dull knowledge-acquisition phase to get there.

Unfortunately, teachers trying to climb the traditional Bloom's cognitive ladder with their students ran into time constraints that frequently kept them from engaging students in analysis, synthesis, and evaluation. Rather than stimulate student minds with higher-level critical thinking skills, they were forced to move on to the next unit to keep with curriculum timelines. The teachers wanted students to think critically—they just didn't have time to do it and meet all of their content requirements.

But what if teachers started with carefully crafted lessons that required students to take a math or science problem, a historic event, or a poem and analyze it to understand some important concept or content? Instead of starting at the bottom of Bloom's Taxonomy, what if these teachers started their students near the top? Rather than lecture (show media or assign reading), what if students had to discover their understanding on their own? Would their learning be more meaningful? Would it be more long lasting?

Traditional Approach to Bloom's Taxonomy: A Ladder Approach -- Students Work Their Way up the Cognitive Ladder

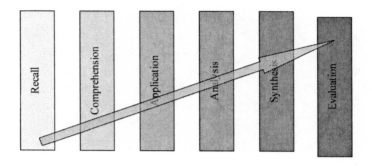

The "Make Kids Think" Approach to Bloom's Taxonomy: Use Higher Level Thinking to Create Lower Level Knowledge and Skills

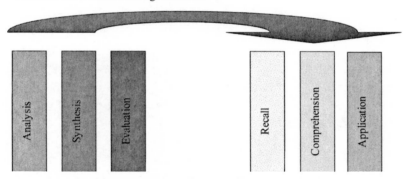

Figure 1.1.   Turning Bloom's Taxonomy on its head.

In the classrooms where students discover their own understanding, teachers have found significant retention and understanding of con-tent—not to mention increased interest in learning. Take, for example, teaching the concepts of theoretical versus experimental probability, which are commonly introduced in elementary mathematics. To try to get students to understand this topic, teachers can employ a didactic strategy and explain the concept outright to students: "If you flip a coin ten times, theoretically you will get heads five times and tails five times. This is called theoretical probability. In real life, which we call experimental probability, you most likely do not get a 50-50 split until you flip a coin many, many times."

If you follow this method of instruction, the concept is taught to students, they practice it with thirty or so problems, and the class can move on to the next lesson. But has this concept been learned in a way students deeply understand and will remember?

If teachers want to make students think and construct their own understanding, however, they change from "sage on the stage" (a dispenser of knowledge) to a facilitator of understanding. In the case of elementary-age probability, the teacher might start by showing the students a penny and asking them what might result if the coin is flipped 10 times. The teacher would let students ponder this idea in small groups. During whole-class sharing that would follow, the teacher would post the students' theories either on the board or under a document camera. The teacher would give students the opportunity to thoroughly explain their thinking.

Next, the teacher would have students flip their coins 100 times in groups then post their results for the class to see (students rarely will get a perfect 50-50 split). Someone would tally the class results for analysis as well. Next, using probing questions, the teacher might ask his or her students to explain why a slight variation of results exists (this would be a good time to introduce the terms experimental and theoretical probability).

By using probing questioning strategies, a teacher can lead students to their own understanding of the difference between theoretical probability, experimental probability, and the concept of probability itself. From here, the teacher can have students transfer their understanding of probability to other things, like dice.

Now, some may ask, why wouldn't the instructor explain the concepts of theoretical and experimental probability first, then have students support their understanding of the concept with an experiment? The teachers could, but it wouldn't be as effective as the discovery method.

The first reason for this is because in classrooms, teachers should have students think as much as possible. Secondly, they want to create an environment with the best chance of information being retained. If teachers want students to function at high levels of Bloom's Taxonomy, the discovery method described above uses *analysis* and *synthesis* to create solidly embedded *knowledge*. But if theoretical and experimental probability were explained to students first, teachers would conduct experiments to support the concept and student thinking would remain at the *knowledge* and *application* level. They really aren't thinking at higher levels.

In the discovery method, students create a hypothesis, conduct an experiment, identify trends, draw conclusions from them, and, if necessary, revise their conclusions. When one thinks about it, isn't that the way adults solve most problems in life?

Finally, if teachers really want student to *think* as much as possible, shouldn't tests and quizzes (both formative and summative) require students to think as well? Many unit tests require a great deal of recall: name the historical event, define the scientific term, identify a character, etc., in a matching-answer, fill-in-the-blank, or short-answer format. Memorization will allow students to pass the test.

Certainly students will not meet educational standards if they don't have a functioning level of memorized content knowledge, but isn't the best test of that knowledge the students' ability to apply it to new situations? Shouldn't a summative assessment be an opportunity to apply their knowledge rather than just recall it?

Creating assessments that really reveal student understanding requires first a change in philosophy. It requires a shift from students showing us what they can recall to students applying their knowledge to new problems, events, or literature. Through this application, teachers assess student knowledge and skills.

In physics, this might mean applying knowledge of negative acceleration to an automobile-accident scene. In social studies, it might mean applying the lessons from the inflated stock-market values of the late 1920s to similar bubbles in 2000 and 2008. In English class, this might mean taking knowledge of parallel structure acquired through the analysis of Martin Luther King's "I Have a Dream" speech and applying it to dissecting John F. Kennedy's inaugural address. In each of these cases, teachers can still assess student content knowledge, but they do so through their capacity to analyze and synthesize (higher-level thinking) rather than their ability to *recall* (lower-level thinking).

While this method of evaluation may take more time to correct than a typical short-answer or matching test, this style of testing engages students and is, in fact, a rewarding experience for teachers as well.

The Reflective Teacher

- How do my students gain their content knowledge in my classroom? What percentage is through textbook reading or lectures? What percentage is through lessons where students gather their knowledge through activities I create?
- If someone were to review one of my assessments, how much of this test would require recall of information? How much would be student use of content knowledge applied to the analysis of new material?

ENCOURAGE FLEXIBLE THINKING

If teachers are to prepare students to function in the real world, they must embrace the fact that often multiple solutions to problems exist— and that a variety of ways to arrive at those solutions may exist. Many of today's teachers were educated in the era of "the one right answer" in schools. There was one way to complete a math problem, one interpretation of a poem. History usually had a correct answer because students were required to know so many dates.

One sign of mature thinking, though, is flexibility: A variety of solutions often exists for problems and each of these solutions has merits on its own. One person's ideas could be right, and another's could be equally correct too.

While certainly there are correct answers and processes that are more efficient than others, teachers do a disservice to students when they overemphasize these in their classroom. In the end, creating learning environments where one right answer is the norm produces students who are misfits to reality. The same is true if teachers insist there is only one process for finding an answer. True, there are cases where only one answer exists; sometimes only one process will arrive at the answer. For the most part, though, these are a minority in the everyday world.

Take a look at the experience of shopping for a new television. While shopping, the consumer might consider picture quality, price, warranty, and a number of other features. When all this is considered, he or she might narrow the field down to two televisions and make a choice between them. Another shopper, however, might consider different criteria (possibly the size or color of the set to fit the decorating needs of a particular room) and narrow his or her decision down to different brands. People often use different processes to solve issues, and often, more than one good solution exists. That is the reality of the world. Shouldn't that be true in classrooms as well?

The philosophy of honoring multiple avenues to an answer creates more engaging learning environments in contemporary math classrooms. In this process, a math problem is given, and students, often in groups, get to work to solve it. When they are finished, students share their work using the document camera for the class to view. The students who share must explain the process by which they arrived at the answer. The teacher facilitates the discussion of the strategies through which the answer was derived. Other students can ask questions.

What students learn—aside from math skills—is that there are often multiple avenues to solving a math problem. They also get to experience the variety of methods other students invent to get their answers.

Take, for example, a real-world application of volume that is tucked cleverly into a landscaping problem. Previous to this math assignment, students study volume of rectangular prisms (rectangular or square boxes), so they are versed on using measurements to calculate volume.

Volume in the real world, though, does not always fit into a neat little box. For this problem, students are given a landscaping schematic on graph paper, where a house is sited near the center of the property. The house is surrounded by a driveway, a walkway, a deck, and curving, irregular-shaped gardens (see Figure 1.2). On the graph paper, each square represents one square foot. The problem that was presented to the students working in collaborative groups is this: If the owner adds bark to the garden areas to a depth of three inches, approximately how many cubic yards of bark need to be purchased for the project at $10 a cubic yard? Calculate your order and how much it will cost.

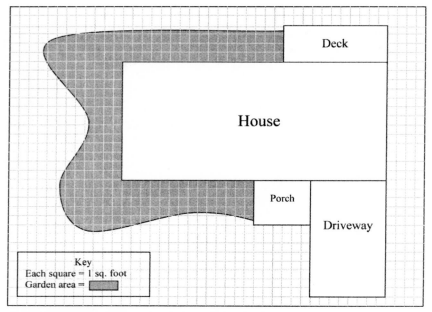

Figure 1.2. *Determining the volume of bark needed.*

For students to compute the volume of bark needed, they first need to calculate the area of the garden space. With students used to dealing with neat geometric shapes, having a curving line run through a one-square-foot box presents challenges for estimating square footage, but figuring out a way to solve this is left to the groups. Should partial squares be combined to try to create whole ones? Should less than a half square of garden space be counted a zero but more than a half be counted as a full one, figuring this will average out in the end? When the groups share out, other students see that numerous different processes are employed to estimate the area of partial squares. As a class, students discuss which methods were more accurate.

Of course, the most accurate method for estimating the area of the garden might not be the most expedient, which leads to a discussion about which method is best for a landscaping-business application where taking time estimating bark deliveries costs money too. In the end, a reasonable range of estimates are correct and a variety of viable processes exist to create that estimate.

By sharing their processes, student not only find different ways to arrive at an answer, they realize that no single "best way" exists to solve this problem. At the same time, in discovering that some methods may be better and more accurate than others, students learn important math skills from their peers.

What is the impact of conducting classes like this? Believing that more than "one right answer exists," more students typically feel free to participate. They feel more empowered. Through large-group sharing, everyone's thinking and ideas are honored (often, "struggling" students, good problem solvers in their own right, start to shine). Thinking and creativity flourish. Students of varying abilities can all work together and learn from one another. Students don't feel the pressure of working alone, and they engage in an activity rather that retreat from it.

A similar approach can be as easily used in analysis of text—say, the study of poetry. Literary analysis need not be an exercise in identifying the single correct interpretation (students trying to figure out the ideas residing in the textbook's teacher edition); rather, poetry study can be an activity where students work as a class to understand difficult text.

This is analysis at its finest: Key words and phrases are analyzed in small groups for meaning, then students explain the interpretation their group drew from them to the class. This collective sharing may lead to a variety of interpretations for a passage, but it also lends itself to good discussion about what makes an interpretation viable or not. This method of poetry study can be particularly satisfying for teachers: They gain a deeper understanding of poems by looking at the variety of interpretations students bring to passages.

Most of adult life is filled with ambiguity, and schools need to prepare students to enter this world. Everyone faces questions in life. What college to attend? Which career choice is the right one? From the complexity of national policy issues to something as simple as selecting a brand of peanut butter, problem solving is rarely clean and simple; one correct answer rarely exists.

If the purpose of education is to produce students who are to function at high levels in a constantly changing world, why create learning environments that run contrary to reality? Yet schools have done just this. The "one answer" or "one process" ethic should make way, whenever appropriate, to a system that embraces the myriad of possible solutions and processes, thus aligning education with the reality of an ambiguous world.

The Reflective Teacher

- How often do students look for "the one right answer" in my classroom?
- How often do I give students the opportunity to share the variety of ways they used to find an answer?
- Where do I create activities where students experience the "ambiguity of life"?

SHIFT TO FINDING KNOWLEDGE

In the last two decades, the explosion that has taken place in accessible information is nearly incomprehensible, and its implications for teaching are far-reaching. High school and college research before the Internet existed often took weeks to complete. The process consisted of thumbing through the card catalog or *Guide to Periodic Literature*, then heading to the stacks to often find the desired source checked out. To make sure the research was solid, a variety of libraries needed to be visited.

Today, students would still be advised to head to libraries for book-length resources, but newspapers and periodicals are easily accessed through the Internet or such services as ProQuest. Using modern resources, students writing a short term paper can complete a search of periodical literature in an evening. Search engines provide the same resources for even the most obscure information.

Such a shift in information availability would naturally spawn a shift in instructional philosophy. Where at one time it might have been appropriate to cram copious amounts of information into a student's head, such is no longer the case. With a seemingly unlimited supply of information easily accessible, does it still make sense for teachers to continue extensive memorization in their classrooms?

This is not to say that basic knowledge is not needed—and shouldn't be considered necessary for graduation. Who could function in life without knowing the multiplication tables? But is it really necessary for future productivity and happiness to be forced to memorize details of an author's life or a novel's minor details if a student doesn't plan to be an English major?

Certainly, it should be expected that students leave school knowing a rough chronological landscape of American history: Declaration of Independence, 1776; the Civil War, mid-1800s; World War I and Woman's Suffrage, early 1900s; etc. But does the average teenager need to attach "1944" to the "Battle of the Bulge" on a fill-in-the-blank test in American-history class?

This is not to argue that there is not basic knowledge in math, science, social studies, and English that every student should know. But long gone should be the days where students memorize information that is easily accessible. While it seems reasonable that students be able to point out the location of states, major rivers, and mountain ranges on a map, the memorization of capitals, state birds, state rock, etc., seems a waste of time when this information is available at a keystroke. Plus, what is the purpose?

A common practice in some Spanish classes, for example, is to memorize the capitals of Central and South American countries—yet how does this make students more fluent or culturally aware? Information is ubiquitous today. Learning how to find it and assess its reliability and bias, however, are thinking skills that need to be taught.

The Reflective Teacher

- To what degree is the information I require students to memorize easily available from other sources?
- How will what I am asking students to memorize aid them as adults?

CHOOSE RIGOROUS CURRICULUM

When educational discussion shifts to raising standards, the words "rigor" or "rigorous" invariably pepper the lexicon of language. An honors class is considered more rigorous than the regular strand because it requires more essays to be written and more novels to be read. A private school may be considered more rigorous than a public one since it requires more hours of homework per week. A lesson that requires students to gather their understanding through research may be described as more rigorous than one where students need to answer a worksheet with facts from a textbook. A Socratic seminar (where a small group of students leads the discussion) may be more rigorous than the standard large-group discussion since it requires students to participate individually to a greater degree.

Looking at the examples above, rigor has a variety of definitions. Rigor can mean more effort, higher cognition, or more engagement. Rigor is one of the most important words in educational reform today. Strangely, though, the word means different things to different groups and different educators. Coming to a common definition of rigor helps teachers in their efforts to make kids think.

If teachers want to make kids think, the terms "rigor" or "rigorous" should apply to the curriculum they present students. In *Teaching What Matters Most: Standards and Strategies for Raising Student Achievement*, Richard Strong, Harvey F. Silver, and Matthew J. Perini define rigor not as workload or a high level of cognition but as the quality of content teachers bring to the curriculum. "Rigor is the goal of helping students develop the capacity to understand content that is *complex, ambiguous, provocative, and personally or emotionally challenging*," they state.[1]

If teachers talk about a rigorous curriculum, they should refer to the *quality* of materials or activities required. Rigor is not higher-level Bloom's Taxonomy: analysis, synthesis, or evaluation. Rigorous activities or materials are the catalyst that sparks higher levels of thinking. To differentiate again between these two vital terms:

- Rigor refers to the quality and engagement level of the content.
- Bloom's Taxonomy measures the cognitive level of brain function when students are engaged in this content.

The differences between these two are subtle but important. They also speak to the importance of good content. Some content or activities will not provoke thoughtful responses, engagement, or high levels of

MAKE KIDS THINK   15

cognition, no matter what teachers do with it. If teachers want to make students think, they need to be very selective in the content and activities they present to them.

Rigorous Curriculum Can Be Complex

Complex material, for example, may have layers of understanding or connectivity to other ideas or concepts. For example, the Dust Bowl is often breezed over in social-studies classes as an unavoidable manmade natural disaster, but this ecological disaster has very complex roots. When studying the causes of the Dust Bowl (Timothy Egan's award-winning *The Worst Hard Time* is an excellent resource), students learn that land in the Great Plains was plowed up in massive quantities to produce food to supply a European farm economy crippled after World War I. European scarcity inflated grain prices to record levels, and farmers, led by the promises of riches, purchased more farm equipment on credit and plowed more grassland for production. When European farms recovered, supply increased, prices fell—and Midwest farmers were forced to till even more land to sell more lower-priced grain just to break even and pay their debts. Then the Midwest's worst drought of the century hit.

The Dust Bowl was not an isolated event, but one that interacts and overlaps with other events of the early 20th century. That North America's greatest ecological disaster has economic roots in Europe is a complex concept. Simply put: no World War I, no Dust Bowl. But how many American-history classes delve deep into its roots?

Similarly, the forces acting on a flying object are very complex and interconnected. Model rocketry becomes an engaging way to synthesize important concepts in physics. To illustrate the complex relationship of a variety of forces, high schools hold model-rocket contests for their physics students.

On the surface, the contest is simple: The team of students has to custom build a rocket, then fly it to a calculated altitude. The teachers provide body tubes of varying diameters, balsa wood fin stock, and nose cones of many shapes and dimensions. Students have a choice of rocket motors of various impulses (power). Concepts of aerodynamic stability, inertia, and drag all need to be accounted for (as well as uncontrollable forces like wind) to loft a model to the calculated altitude, but it can be done.

In one contest, one school team flew to 15 feet and another to 10 feet of their projected altitude. Both, though, were beaten by another school team who flew to three feet of the projected altitude. In this project, concepts of physics interact and overlap. Further, this hands-on project, while very complex, was engaging and fun.

Rigorous Curriculum Can Be Provocative

While some curriculum is complex, other material becomes engaging because it provokes deep thinking and great discussions. When students deal with provocative curriculum, they have to deal with dilemmas, delve into sticky issues, or take moral stands that may run contrary to the mainstream.

Unquestionably, Henry David Thoreau's "On the Duty of Civil Disobedience" is one of the most provocative essays students in high school or college will read.[2] Thoreau refused to pay his taxes because he believed they were going to an unjust war. He spent the night in a Concord jail for his transgression. As a result of his stay in jail, he penned this essay.

The essay's thesis is simple: Do not abide unjust laws or governments. This controversial essay became a philosophical underpinning for nonviolent philosophies of Mahatma Gandhi and Martin Luther King Jr. It literally changed the world.

Thoreau's thesis is extremely controversial (some might say subversive), yet it elicits lively discussion with the prompt: Should citizens follow laws or rules that they deem unjust? That is about as provocative as class discussions can get, yet this concept of holding government to the highest of standards is vital if liberty is to be maintained. When it is appropriate to break unjust laws (think Rosa Parks or the Vietnam protestors) is an extremely provocative intellectual question, but one that needs to be discussed.

Provocative issues surround students, and concepts need not be "lofty" to be engaging. Banning cell phones and text messaging in classrooms, forbidding Halloween costumes in school because other cultures fear witches, ghosts, and goblins, or canceling student mixers because parents and administrators find dance moves "inappropriate" are all fertile ground for classroom discussions and activities. Delving into issues of cloning and genetic engineering adds a twist to the normally "rational" discipline of science.

Provocative issues make excellent topics for persuasive writing assignments. Discussing provocative issues may make some administrators uncomfortable because they stir the pot. Education, though, should not be a passive act. Provocative concepts force students to wade into the moral messiness of adult life. They also engage students and "make kids think."

Rigorous Curriculum Can Be Ambiguous

Student thinking can be brought to a fine edge by searching for meaning in ambiguous material. Ambiguity can be found in great literature, primary documents, charts, and statistics. Whenever material is packed with ambiguity or multiple meanings, students are forced to really think in order to understand its significance.

Students need not be young adults or older to grapple with the ambiguities of life. Depending upon the right instructional material, ambiguity can be approached at a very age-appropriate manner.

The award-winning elementary-age novel *Because of Winn-Dixie* provides an excellent example for young students dealing with ambiguity.[3] In the story, India Opal Buloni (called Opal) adopts a stray dog which she names Winn-Dixie. The town librarian, Miss Fanny Block, befriends Opal, who is the daughter of a preacher and new to town. Besides loaning out her books, Miss Fanny shares the story of her great-grandfather Littmus W. Block, who built the town's once prosperous (now defunct) candy factory, which produced the one-time, world-renowned Littmus Lozenge.

During one visit to the library, Fanny Block tells Opal the story of her grandfather's life. As a fourteen-year-old, Littmus Block enlisted in the Confederate Army. As Fanny says, "He left behind his mother and three sisters." (His father had already enlisted.) "He went off to be a hero. But he soon found out the truth." In the war, he was shot at, covered in fleas and lice, and saw men die.

At the war's end, he longs for the love of his family, but he returns to his Virginia home to find the Yankees have burned it to the ground.

His mother and sisters have died of typhoid fever, and his father was killed on the battlefield. He misses his family and breaks down and "cried just like a baby."

When he is done weeping, he has a desire for something sweet, a piece of candy. Feeling that the world is a sorry place, Fanny's great-grandfather walks from Virginia to Florida, builds a factory, and, determined to add sweetness to the world, creates the Littmus Lozenge. But his candy has a peculiar trait: It tastes of root beer and strawberry—and another indescribable flavor that makes people recall the sadness in their lives. Rather than drive down sales, this characteristic leads the Littmus Lozenge to popularity nationally and worldwide.

Can young schoolchildren understand one of life's great paradoxes, that it can be both sweet and sad at the same time? With the right follow-up activity to the text, they can. At this point in the story, one elementary teacher hands out strawberry and root-beer hard candy. Students float the hard candy atop their tongues and describe what they taste. Immediately, these students "taste" life's sweetness but also its sorrows. "I can taste the sadness of my grandfather dying in the hospital," says one student. "It reminds me of my parents' divorce," remarks another.

Next, students record their thoughts about the book and their lives on graphic organizers shaped like Littmus Lozenge wrappers. To tie the activity to the book, each main character has a wrapper section devoted to them. On one half of the wrapper, students have to analyze the characters' lives for what is sweet. On the other half, they need to identify the sadness. One additional wrapper section is added—students are asked to identify the happiness and the sorrow in their own lives. At an elementary age, few are shy about expressing their feelings honestly.

Because of Winn-Dixie is extremely popular with elementary students, not because it can be broken down into a neat formula—but because it can't. The ambiguity in the novel ties into the reality of the lives kids live. The ambiguity prompts schoolchildren to think about their world. In other words, ambiguity makes kids think.

Rigorous Curriculum Can Be Emotionally or Personally Challenging

Some of the finest learning comes when students are impacted on a personal level—when it makes them ponder how the world really operates.

Most want to believe in an orderly universe and compassionate humans, until they read Elie Wiesel's *Night*.[4] This autobiography about the Holocaust challenges any naive notion people may have that the world, by nature, is orderly and just. In the book, Wiesel and his family are sent to Auschwitz-Birkenau concentration camp, where, he learns years later, his mother and sister were immediately sent to the gas chamber.

Wiesel's and his father's lives are reduced to an existence of hard work and starvation, where thoughts focus on little more than concerns for the next meal. Family bonds break. Sons abandon their weakened fathers. Once, devout inmates are paraded past the body of an executed youth they were forced to watch die and ask themselves, "Where is God now?" Simply put, *Night* is a difficult, emotional read, but it prompts questions about human treatment of one another that are difficult—even impossible—to answer.

Enhancing a "cognitive" discipline like science with an emotionally engaging component adds a dimension that can make kids think about how their studies apply to real life. For example, before classrooms jump into the causes of global warming, students might study the possible impacts: polar bears floundering to keep from drowning due to decreased Arctic ice, large stretches of Colorado forests dead due to increases in bark beetles, photos of Glacier Park devoid of permanent ice sometime in this century. Students want to live on a healthy planet, and studying the impact of global warming—or whether or not global warming exists at all—makes the unit on potential climate change all the more relevant to them.

Defining rigor as the *quality of curriculum* helps educators hone in on a principal challenge in the profession: identifying quality, age-appropriate content for students that "makes kids think."

One of the challenges every teacher faces is keeping students engaged. Often, though, it is not the students who are at fault but the curriculum. Bright, inquisitive minds are shoe-horned into uncreative, unengaging content because it is "good for them," and teachers wonder why they tune out in their classrooms and fail to perform on their tests. The content taught does matter. It's the difference between recalling facts and making kids think. Rigorous content should form the foundation of all classroom activities.

The Reflective Teacher

- To what degree do I *regularly* present provocative, ambiguous, complex, or emotionally engaging curriculum or activities?

MAKE LEARNING RELEVANT

The strategy of Make Kids Think is foundational to a quality classroom experience. To engage students, though, content needs to be as relevant to their lives as possible. Teachers need to create assignments that require thinking yet entice interest.

When teaching the concept of sinusoids in her junior-level math class, one teacher does not rely upon abstract statistics: She goes real world. In order to analyze wave patterns (sinusoids), the adept math teacher has her students download from the Internet the carbon dioxide readings from the volcano Mauna Loa in Hawaii. CO_2 levels rise and fall with the seasons—creating sinusoidal graphs—but the level of this much-talked-about gas in the atmosphere has been steadily on the rise as measured on Mauna Loa since the 1950s.

Mathematics in this lesson is no longer theoretical or irrelevant. Students create equations that model the sinusoidal functions then make predictions about carbon dioxide levels in the future. In the process, these students think about how the atmosphere is changing.

Expert reading teachers use clever, relevant newspaper clippings and magazine headlines to analyze the nuances of language. These teachers use these sophisticated forms of expression successfully with their struggling readers, drawing as much meaning from the students as they can before eliciting greater understanding through carefully crafted questions. Using the news of the day, social-studies teachers can employ political cartoons on topics relevant to the world of their students.

In these student-centered classrooms, the students work collaboratively to identify important elements and decipher the meaning. To infer meaning is a skillful combination of knowledge, analysis, and synthesis—and fun at the same time if the topic is ripe.

Tweaking assignments to make them more relevant to kids' lives dramatically increases student engagement. When teaching compare-contrast writing skills in a high school English class, rather than have students analyze two works of literature (often a typical assignment), teachers can have them compare and contrast two products they would like to buy. Talk about a change in engagement.

Any teacher who has taught compare-contrast writing knows it can be challenging and, to be honest, a dull affair if the topic is not engaging for students. The technical nature of the writing, though, can be softened by teaching and monitoring students' consumer-thinking skills (What about the differences in warranties? One costs less, but are all the features the same?), which are skills adults employ when comparing something as common as cell-phone plans.

Teaching these challenging writing assignments by adding consumerism skills doesn't add much more time to the activity, but it does add relevance and broadens students' compare-contrast thinking skills beyond the academic setting.

If teachers want students to really think, they need to find material that is provocative, ambiguous, complex, or emotionally engaging, *plus* relevant to students' lives. When teachers "make students think," they not only drive home the content and skills they desire but also raise the engagement level in classrooms and prepare students for the real world they are to enter. Relevant material makes learning engaging.

The Reflective Teacher

- How relevant to students' lives are the activities that I regularly teach?
- How can I tweak assignments so that I can make them more engaging and relevant to students' lives?

CLOSING

The job of educators is to make students solid thinkers and problem solvers—to kindle and stoke a flame rather than fill a vessel, as Plutarch suggests in this chapter's opening quote. Where at one time schools were places where large amounts of content were imparted and memorized (a necessity at the time), much of that content is available in seconds at the stroke of a computer or cell-phone key.

Certainly, students need to leave school systems understanding basic scientific concepts, the landscape of history, relevant mathematical algorithms, and the content of cultural literature. This goal, however, can be largely achieved with lessons that have students ponder, analyze, predict, synthesize, and calculate. The trick is to engage students in activities that allow them to discover their own understanding—because that is the process they will employ again and again throughout their lives.

The journey from "sage on the stage" to facilitator of thinking is not an overnight process. To create these lessons and the class environment that sustains them requires not only creativity but a deep understanding of the content to be taught. This transformation requires ingenuity and self-analysis. It takes time. For educators, the process is one of trial and error, but the change in student engagement can be almost immediate.

"Make students think" changes students from passive learners to engaged learners. It reduces dependence on the teacher and creates independent students. It produces students ready to grapple with the challenges and complexity of adult life.

Teach Big Ideas

Ideas matter. They engage. They motivate. They change the world. Think of this statement: "We hold these truths to be self-evident, that all men are created equal, that they are endowed by their Creator with certain unalienable Rights, that among these are Life, Liberty, and the pursuit of Happiness." Thirty-five words. Yet the idea these words embody had the power to fuel the American Revolution and change the design of world governments forever.

Consider the concept of Manifest Destiny. Believing America should stretch from ocean to ocean, over 200,000 pioneers joined wagon trains and trudged across half a continent to build a better life. The concept populated the West with people of European and Asian descent in a few generations. This idea altered forever American Indian culture.

Ideas have tremendous power. They direct lives, oftentimes determining actions without individuals consciously knowing it. New ideas can dramatically redirect lives. "Bigger is better" is a concept that drove Americans to build mini-mansions and drive gas-guzzling trucks and SUVs—until the price of energy went through the ceiling and global temperatures began to rise. The concern over potential global warming and higher fuel costs are spawning a more earth-friendly ethic. Due to a change in thinking, citizens seek public transportation and fuel-efficient vehicles. Rather than waste, they recycle. Homes are designed to require less energy.

A simple concept like stewardship of the earth and economy of financial resources can transform billions of human lives.

Ideas matter, and big ideas chart the course of society and lives. If schools are to be the creators of a common culture, those ideas that make better, more effective individuals and citizens need to be front and center in the curriculum. But are big life-changing ideas now at the heart of efforts to educate children and youth?

TRADITIONAL TEACHING VERSUS BIG IDEAS

Whether it is mathematical algorithms, scientific formulas, or rules of grammar, education traditionally is seen as the sum of the content or skills students take away from a school or a university. For example, a traditional way to teach history is to use a chronological approach. Given the fact that history unfolds over decades and centuries, this may seem to be a very appropriate approach given that one era leads to the next, and the events that shape one age have consequences for those that follow.

Many who have a great love for history believe that a certain level of historical background knowledge is important to be a contributor to a democratic society. Santayana's saying "He who forgets the past is doomed to repeat it" is a fundamental truth. If society doesn't learn from past mistakes, it will make them again.

A certain level of historical, mathematical, and scientific content literacy is necessary to understand and function in the modern world.

The challenge schools face, though, when they teach strictly content (whether this be science, mathematics, language arts, or history) is retention of factual knowledge. In order to make the content manageable, teachers for regular social-studies students, for example, must either reduce the content to core events or eras and study them well (as AP students or history majors do in college) or cover many different eras or events but at a lesser depth, a sampler approach. What often happens in either method is that history is reduced to a series of facts that students are asked to memorize.

The problem, though, is that for most students, history becomes a series of disjointed details, memorized for the test (if the teacher is lucky) and then often forgotten.

Take the Lewis and Clark expedition, for example. In a well-respected AP American-history text, the Lewis and Clark expedition is reduced to less than a page of text. The book attributes numerous scientific discoveries to the aptly named Corps of Discovery, discusses Lewis's brush with death during a deadly conflict with Blackfoot scouts, and credits the explorers with finding a way to the Pacific, all of which are important.

For a teacher who comes from the Pacific Northwest, where counties, towns, rivers, and schools are named after members of this party, though, the text's narrative on the expedition is limited, but given all the American history the publisher attempts to cover in one book, the narrow coverage is understandable. To get the major events covered, history is reduced to a narrow series of dates and events, often organized around eras.

While history buffs are fascinated by how the Corps of Discovery was the first known group of American citizens to cross the West, chronicle its flora, fauna, and landscape, and return, the deeper story of the Lewis and Clark expedition is much more compelling. In fact, what made the Corps of Discovery successful is fertile ground for students to explore big ideas relevant to their lives, among them:

- How does teamwork lead to success?
- What makes for successful leadership?
- What role does luck play in life?

For those who delve into the history of the expedition, the answers to these questions are what fascinate them because they are still so contemporary. Needless to say, the questions asked above cannot be gleaned from a page of text in a history book. Identifying leadership skills and teamwork requires students to read and research selected excerpts from books, the Lewis and Clark journals, and the Internet. Identifying good luck requires focused study of Sacagawea meeting her brother by chance at Camp Fortunate and the Nez Perce befriending—rather than massacring—the explorers after they emerged near death from the Bitterroot Mountains.

Without teamwork, leadership, and luck, the Lewis and Clark expedition would not have been successful. Studying the expedition to this depth obviously takes much longer than the textbook writers intend, but delving into the Corps of Discovery at this depth can be greatly beneficial to students.

When students can take lessons from the Lewis and Clark expedition and apply them to their own lives, they see the relevance of their studies. The expedition no longer remains lumps of information that students see as something "teachers think we should know." Creating lessons and units around big ideas is very much about relevance. It's about studying content and building skills around core big ideas that matter.

ENDURING UNDERSTANDINGS AND ESSENTIAL QUESTIONS

Knowingly or unknowingly, great teachers have focused their instruction around big ideas, but credit for bringing this concept to collective professional teaching consciousness goes to Grant Wiggins and Jay McTighe. Their book *Understanding by Design* reoriented the way many educators view teaching, and it places the concept of big ideas in the forefront of curriculum development.[1]

Rather than using the term "big ideas," *Understanding by Design* refers to them as Enduring Understandings (EUs) and frames their study through Essential Questions (EQs). EUs are meant to be "forty-year learnings," meaning that students can apply this knowledge for the next four decades of their lives and beyond. Enduring Understandings are big ideas. An EU for the Lewis and Clark expedition might be "Teamwork is essential for success." This EU applies to the Corps of Discovery, but it could also apply equally to aspects of the lives of elementary, middle school, and high school students, as well as military generals, school administrators, and CEOs. It has a life of 40 years and beyond.

Enduring Understandings of big ideas are translated into Essential Questions, which guide student study. In the case of the Lewis and Clark expedition, students would be given Essential Questions to guide their study: "How does teamwork lead to success?" Note how this Essential Question is so big it could relate to football and national politics as well as Lewis and Clark. (The general nature of Enduring Understandings are by design—they are meant to be broad in nature and relevant to life.)

Whether teachers call them big ideas or Enduring Understandings, significant concepts have the power to create long-term learning.

The Reflective Teacher

- How purposefully are my lessons designed around some big concept that gives my students relevant, long-term understanding?

MAKE LEARNING STICK WITH BIG IDEAS

No matter what discipline of learning, studying topics around "big ideas" leads to better retention. According to the groundbreaking book *How People Learn: Brain, Mind, Experience, and School,* Principle 2 states, "To develop competence in an area of inquiry, learners must (a) have a deep foundation of factual knowledge, (b) *understand facts and ideas in the context of a conceptual framework*; and (c) *organize knowledge in ways that facilitate retrieval and application.*" [emphasis added][2] In other words, facts need to be understood within the context of bigger concepts if they are to be retained.

If teachers think about their own learning, this makes sense. How often are adults given random information only to have it slip from their mind hours later? In schools and colleges, students cram for tests only to forget the information in weeks.

Learning is like lint. Unless it clings to something, it drifts off and is gone. Rather than have students remember a list of unrelated events, teachers should organize their learning around lasting concepts. In the end, good classroom instruction and discovery should create a lasting, retrievable knowledge base and, when possible, build wisdom in students as well.

The big ideas for a science or math unit or a lesson can be content driven and relevant to life as well. For example, in a unit created to study dissolved chemicals and gases, a group of middle school science teachers embedded student learning in studying the water quality of the river that runs through their city.

For the experiments, they assigned students the role of being members of a research team hired to analyze the current state of the river.

Their purpose was to hunt for possible polluters: farms in the watershed, golf courses, a paper mill, and the wastewater-treatment plant. Teachers chose this topic because river quality had become of great importance in their community.

For this series of experiments, teachers fetched water samples from various spots along the river to study changes in water quality and hunt down possible sources of pollution. Students used probes and sensors to measure the water level of acidity, dissolved oxygen, phosphates, and other chemicals.

Next, using the data gathered, the students attempted to identify the largest point (a paper factory or sewage-disposal plant, for example) and nonpoint polluters (fertilizer flushed in via streams from surrounding golf courses or farms) of the river. Their final product for the unit came in the form of a fictitious report to the state's Department of Ecology, identifying sources of pollution and recommendations for improving river quality.

For this science unit, a big idea dealt with scientific concepts: "The environment is a system of interconnected parts that continually and consistently influence each other." A second big idea dealt with stewardship of the environment: "Human activities and choices affect natural resources and may impact the health of the environment (in this case the river)."

In effect, the study of the river made students better scientists and more enlightened citizens. The scientific learning had more relevance and greater long-term retention because it was attached to a topic of local concern and media attention. After the experiment, students could explain to their parents the impact of dissolved chemicals and gasses on the river the next time the issue of its water quality was covered in the media.

By tying chemistry to river stewardship, studying chemicals and gases dissolved in water was no longer an abstract concept. What students learned from their experiments had relevance to their lives and, therefore, was better retained.

Contrast this with how the unit might normally be taught. In a traditional lab setting, students might receive beakers of mystery solutions (mixed previously in the lab by the teacher) where they would use probes and sensors to measure the qualities of the water. They might also receive distilled water, add the minerals and gases themselves, then write lab reports containing their results. Scientific concepts about water absorption would be learned, but there would be little connection to applying science to the world around them.

The difference between the two water-quality units is that the traditional method dealt only with scientific concepts, while teachers' studying actual river water intentionally dealt with scientific concepts tied to relevant, applicable big ideas.

As mentioned in the previous chapter, a high school math teacher was attaching the study of sinusoids (graphs of waves) to the concept of global warming years before Al Gore's *An Inconvenient Truth* hit the theaters. A mathematical big idea for that lesson might be "Data can be graphed and formulas created for regularly occurring phenomenon." But a more relevant big idea is "CO_2 levels in the atmosphere have been steadily climbing since the 1950s."

In a traditional classroom, students would be learning mathematical formulas in isolation. By attaching content to a big idea—in this case the concept of rising levels of CO_2—students are learning important mathematical content in terms of an issue critical to their future. In addition, by tying sinusoids to the concept of global warming, students are more likely to understand and retain the importance of this mathematical concept.

The key to keeping lessons focused around big ideas is to refer back regularly to the essential questions posed in the lesson or unit. Essential questions should be posted in the classroom and reviewed as students progress through the unit. The degree to which students can answer the essential questions is a useful tool to assess how they are progressing in the unit.

Making understanding of the unit's or lesson's big-idea part of the final assessment or performance task synthesizes student understanding of the concepts that need to be taught. For example, teachers might end a mini-unit on the Lewis and Clark expedition described above with either an essay test or a project that reflects upon a big idea for study: "Teamwork leads to success." Questions that prompt a writing reflection or a final project might be as follows:

- "To what degree was teamwork a vital component of the Lewis and Clark expedition?" (analysis), and

- "Identify one area of your life where teamwork is essential. Using the Corps of Discovery as a model, explain how you might improve your role as a member of that team?" (Relevant analysis of students' lives and synthesis of content taken from the unit.)

The two prompts presented above have the power to pull together student learning of the content presented.

For the water-quality unit, teachers might end with a question or a project based on the prompt, "What might our community do to be better stewards of our river?"

The final prompts, whether they are answered in an essay or a project, have the power to pull content together around a big idea and make it stick. For big ideas to work, though, they need to function as mileposts that teachers use to monitor student understanding through the unit as well as a tool for summative assessments.

Teaching using "big ideas" in no way undermines or negates the importance of teaching content. In fact, big ideas allow for the creation of a web of conceptual understanding that leads to retention of content as *How People Learn*'s Principle 2 suggests.

The Reflective Teacher

- What are the big ideas in the units I currently teach?
- Are the lessons designed so the big ideas can be transferred to students' lives?

ARE STANDARDS HIGH ENOUGH?

Unfortunately, big ideas are not necessarily tied to the standards-based movement. Standards are most often skills—not the big, mind-altering ideas that direct or redirect student lives. For example, when you examine writing standards at the ninth-grade level, they might read something like, "Revises text, including changing words, sentences, paragraphs, and ideas." For reading, one standard might be, "Synthesizes information from a variety of sources."

Social-studies standards might call for knowledge of how government functions and civic participation, but they lack clear, big ideas for students to follow. For example, one Washington state standard reads, "The student understands and applies knowledge of government, law, politics, and the nation's fundamental documents to make decisions about local, national, and international issues and to demonstrate thoughtful, participatory citizenship."[3]

This is exactly what one dimension of social studies ought to do, but it doesn't provide succinct, clear, big ideas that guide students in life, such as a big idea like "Democracies function well only when the electorate is educated on issues" might. Reviewing mathematics and science bring the same results; most state standards are concepts or skills, not life-changing ideas.

There is no argument that teaching skills, content, and conceptual understanding should be a primary function of schools. These provide students with the ability to function effectively in their world. If students lack essential reading, writing, and basic mathematical skills, or fail to understand certain scientific concepts, they simply handicap their future.

With content standards now set by grade level in states, teachers know what skills need to be taught when. This is a major step forward in education, yet it also has created a dark side. One problem with standards-based education is the narrowing effect it can have on teachers and administrators.

Standards are tangible, something firm to hang on to in a profession that deals with all too many intangible elements. Standards can be assigned to curriculum. The level of success can be measured. Results can be analyzed. Teaching becomes mathematical. The frenzy to meet standards, though, can spawn a kind of myopia: The most important thing in schools becomes meeting standards. Most standards are skills- or content/concept-based, meaning their intent is to make students better human machines. Fully productive human lives, though, are more complex than this.

What if educators took the teaching of those skills and core concepts to be the sole goal of instruction in their classroom as the standards-based movement proposes? Imagine if a football coach strictly followed this concept and concerned himself with teaching his young players only skills and strategies. He might produce a state-championship team, but he has forgotten that the playfield should be teaching important life lessons, among them: function as a team to be successful; keep a positive attitude in the face of defeat; and drive and diligence pay dividends (none of which technically are skills or game concepts).

Few parents expect their sons or daughters to be professional athletes. They want them to be healthy, productive adults. When it comes to athletics, most would agree that important life lessons like those mentioned above are at least as important as throwing a perfect spiral or running a precise passing pattern. As a parent, these "life lessons" are the "big ideas."

In the quest for excellence, schools, like an overambitious coach bent on statistics and victories, run the risk of forgetting the "big picture" as well.

How does this play out in a classroom? A canon of early high school is the teaching of Harper Lee's *To Kill a Mockingbird*.[4] In this unit, the following skills (standards) can be taught. Students are to:

- Identify the main idea of the selection and support their choice with details from the text.
- Build upon the prior knowledge they bring to the text.
- Summarize passages.
- Analyze for similarities and differences.
- Synthesize information from a variety of sources.
- Analyze text to draw conclusions and develop insights.
- Analyze and evaluate ideas and concepts within, among, and beyond multiple texts.

These are excellent literary-analysis skills and a major step-up from the all-too-common recall mentality in classrooms. In fact, these are skills that should be taught for any work of literature. If students were nothing more that machines to be taught to think, these would do the trick. But students are not machines; they are mind, body, and soul.

One of *Mockingbird*'s timeless qualities is the humble, honest, and heroic traits of its protagonist, Atticus Finch. He is one of American's finest literary heroes and a powerful role model for students. When his children define manhood as the ability to shoot accurately or play football, Atticus redirects their thinking: He helps them redefine courage not as "a man with a gun" but as someone who fights for the right cause, knowing he may lose. Atticus defies the sentiment of the southern 1930's town and defends African American Tom Robinson against a rape charge, an extremely unpopular stand in the fictional town of Maycomb.

One big idea that emerges from the novel is "Sometimes doing the right thing may be unpopular." Another big idea is "Never judge people until you see life from their point of view." Both of these big ideas are tremendously relevant to students' lives. They have the power to create not only lively discussions, but also to transform how young people act and view life. Certainly, working to imbue students' lives with these two big ideas is at least as important a task as honing their literary skills.

Skills allow people to function in life, but ideals encompassed in big ideas are what direct their lives and give them meaning. Life-directing ideas like these need to be front and center when teachers talk curriculum. In a skills-based environment, there is the potential for less educational effort being placed on the concepts that serve students' inner compass when they navigate life.

What is needed is to balance the drive to meet standards with big ideas that help students understand the world and make them fully functioning, compassionate, moral human beings. This in no way means reducing efforts to get students to meet standards. Instead, it mandates that teachers take special care to round out the curriculum to teach both standards and worthy big ideas.

Big ideas need to be central to curriculum. Students need to grapple with them, understand them, and apply them as if their lives depend upon them—because the quality of their lives does.

Lewis and Clark could be taught as a set of facts—or made into lessons on leadership. Water analysis can be a simple chemistry experiment—or it can be reformatted to teach science concepts *and* stewardship of a valuable local resource. A math lesson can focus on creating a formula—or it can teach the concept of sinusoids within a very valuable lesson on rising CO_2 levels.

Each day, teachers make choices. They can teach skills and standards in isolation—or they can find ways to tie lessons to valuable, real-life big ideas.

The Reflective Teacher

- How do the lessons I teach tie to students' lives outside my class-room?
- To what degree do the lessons I teach contain ideas that will better the character of my students or improve their ability to understand and function in the world?

THE POWER OF BIG IDEAS IN DAILY TEACHING PRACTICE

Identifying big ideas and creating lessons that both teach these concepts *and* meet required standards can be a transformative experience for teachers. When designing lessons or units, teachers first sort through the state standards that need to be met for the lesson or unit. Next, they look to the curriculum and the big ideas that might emerge.

Identifying a potential big idea and articulating it in a way students will understand and apply it to their lives can be a challenging task. When working collaboratively, linking standards to big ideas can lead to in-depth discussions among teachers about what core concepts need to be taught. These discussions can be dynamic and thought provoking. Teachers become intimate with both their standards and their content.

Finding a core idea can be a struggle, but identification leads to unity of purpose. Everyone has written essays for high school or college and knows the challenge that comes with identifying the appropriate thesis. When the thesis is finally refined, the remainder of the essay falls easily into place. The purpose of the paper becomes clear: That which supported the thesis was retained or expanded in the essay; ideas that ran contrary were discarded. Identifying the big ideas for a set of standards focuses lessons in a similar way. Big ideas add clarity to what needs to be taught.

Entities outside education wrestle with big, unifying ideas, too. Companies, organizations, and individuals work to identify their core purpose when they create mission statements. They sort through the myriad of things they do to identify the core concepts that define them. Mission statements are big ideas that provide clarity of purpose that directs actions, work, and decision making.

Identifying the big idea for a lesson is similar. Once this focus is achieved, the teachers become clear about what they need to teach and why. Lessons and units become attached to a bigger cause. Skills being taught have a context for their use. When teachers present their lessons, they stay on track because the big idea, like a compass, becomes an idea to guide them. Meeting and measuring standards becomes part of larger learning.

In efforts to teach to standards, educators perhaps sometimes forget that the purpose of school is to prepare students to function in all aspects of life. How is the best way to accomplish this? Teach big ideas that are relevant to students' lives. Educators can meet standards and teach big ideas at the same time.

TEASING BIG IDEAS FROM STANDARDS

As a high school history teacher, Susie Gerard is anything but traditional. Rather than desks lined in rows, students work collaboratively at tables. Course textbooks are used, but they are not the primary source for information. Students learn through WebQuests, individual research, performance tasks, and collaborative small-group discussions.

History may be a dry topic to many students, but there is no boredom in her classroom. Gerard delivers a full class period of engagement. Day in and day out, Gerard presents lessons that make kids think. Gerard is also a believer in the power of teaching big ideas, those concepts that shape students into productive adults who will participate responsibly in the democratic process. She strives to find big ideas that both capture the essence of the content and are relevant to students' lives.

In her 12th-grade European history AP course, students spend one unit studying key political philosophers from the early modern European period, which ran from 1600 to 1750. The writings studied come from John Locke, Thomas Hobbes, Niccolo Machiavelli, James I, and Frederick the Great. The ideas espoused by these thinkers heavily influenced the creation of the political systems—and the ethics—that drive governments today.

The 12th-grade Washington state standards (GLEs) that guide the study of the early modern European period unit are as follows:[5]

- Civics 1.1.2: Understands the purposes, organization, and function of governments, laws, and political systems.

- History 4.4.3: Understands that there are multiple perspectives and interpretations of historical events.
- Social Studies Skills 5.5.1: Uses critical reasoning skills to analyze and evaluate positions.

Further, AP standards direct teachers to look at historical periods and address these themes:[6]

- Intellectual, cultural, and political developments and their relationship to social values and political events.
- Developments in social, economic, and political thought, including ideologies characterized as "-isms," such as socialism, liberalism, nationalism.
- The rise and functioning of the modern state in its various forms.
- Changes in political thought and institutions.
- The extension and limitation of rights and liberties (personal, civic, economic, and political).

If followed precisely, the standards listed above will build analytic skills and civic and historic content. Nowhere, though, is there a specific standard or big idea that transforms the way students view their world.

From these standards, though, Gerard develops learning that transforms students' thinking. Gerard's goal is for students to develop civic competence in terms of their understanding of their role in a democratic nation, refine their own beliefs about the role of government and the law, and analyze the relationship between modern world leaders and the law.

Her objective is to not only prepare students for the AP test, but to develop their civic competence and social understanding. She wants these students of voting or near voting age ready to participate in the political life of society.

The big ideas that Gerard has teased from these standards and content to guide and shape student understanding for the unit are directed by these essential questions:

- "What is your role in a democratic society?"
- "What is the purpose of law and the government?"

- "How much power should a political leader have?" "Is anyone—including a leader—above the law?"

To lead her students toward formulating their beliefs (Gerard does not provide answers to these questions), she has them carefully prepare for a class debate where they will wrestle with these big ideas. To create a knowledge base, Gerard uses a jigsaw activity.

To begin this activity, she divides her students into five groups. Each group will study the work of one writer: Locke, Hobbes, Machiavelli, James I, or Frederick the Great. In these groups, students read text from the common writer and then discuss his ideas until they understand the content well. Students are expected to become "experts" on the core concepts and philosophies of their group's assigned writer, their piece of the jigsaw puzzle. This prepares them for the next activity, where they put all the pieces together.

Next, these students join a second collaborative group, where this time each member represents a *different* writer. Students share the key points of their own political writer with their group. Like a jigsaw puzzle, students, through their sharing, fit all these concepts together to create an understanding of European political thinking from 1600 to 1750.

Gerard asks her students in groups to compare and contrast the ideas of the philosophers regarding the role of government and definitions of ideals (such as liberty). Next, based on the reading, they are asked to analyze how a person's beliefs about human nature and social factors (such as wars, economic status, gender, intellectual trends, etc.) influence their beliefs about government. In the process, they are asked to cultivate a political philosophy of their own based on these writers to answer the essential questions: "What is the purpose of law and the government?" and "What is your role in a democratic society?"

Debating how these writers' ideas have relevance to today synthesizes student understanding. Students conclude the unit with this spirited debate to answer, "How much power should a political leader have?" and "Is anyone—including a leader—above the law?"

The concepts of this unit, directed by the hunt for big-idea answers to essential questions, help to shape student beliefs and prepare them for participation in the political process of their community, state, and nation. This unit engages students because its big ideas are relevant to their lives.

The Reflective Teacher

- How do the lessons I teach either confirm or revise my students' view of themselves and the world around them?

CLOSING

In this standards-based age, it is easy to dismiss the big picture and become entrenched in meeting only skills and course content and concepts—thus making the educational energy focused on meeting state-mandated assessments. The irony, though, is that by maintaining a narrow focus on meeting standards, believing they are the only "true north," teachers may be partially failing their students. While thinking that they are preparing them for life, they may be leaving them only partially equipped to function as adults.

Educators are called to a higher duty: to create students of well-rounded intellect and character. Yes, teachers need to meet standards with their students, but they must also fulfill a higher calling: tying curriculum to big ideas and concepts that are relevant to students' lives and their futures.

Schools should be places that impart life wisdom. They should be places that either confirm or challenge who students are, what they believe, and how they will live their lives in this very complex world. To accomplish this, students need to wrestle with big ideas.

Ideas matter. They inspire. They direct. They transform. If teachers' duty is to build well-rounded individuals, their task is to teach big ideas.

Nurture Student Learning

Whoever would one day learn to fly must first learn to stand and walk and run and climb and dance; one cannot fly into flying.

—Fredrick Nietzsche

Set in early 1900's Montana, the movie *A River Runs Through It* not only depicts the sport of fly-fishing in cinematic beauty, it provides a powerful teaching model for educators. The boys' father, Reverend Maclean, an accomplished fly fisherman, was serious about his boys becoming adept fly casters themselves. Reverend Maclean did not leave the instruction of proper fly casting to chance. He was very precise in his methodology. He directed his two sons to cast using a four-count rhythm.

To enforce the count, he trains his sons to cast, using a metronome. With the metronome balanced atop a fence post, tapping out a rhythm, the two young boys practice their casting motions while a stoic father looks on, critiquing. As a result of the structured technique and fatherly oversight, the two boys become adept at fly casting.

Later in the story, though, something magical happens to an adult Paul Maclean. Having mastered his father's structured method, he advances beyond his childhood instruction and fashions a casting style of his own: shadow casting. At the climax of the movie, Paul hooks a giant trout using this method, fights and eventually lands the fish, prompting his normally stoic father to exclaim "You are a *fine* fisherman"—the greatest compliment he would receive from his normally reserved parent.

The story of Paul Maclean's rise to fly-fishing mastery is a power-ful illustration for effective instruction. To start his boys' growth to-ward fly-fishing mastery, the Reverend Maclean taught his sons skills based on knowable criteria for success: casting strokes to a four-count rhythm. For a model for instruction, the boys looked no further than their father for technique. Next, the boys were given ample practice time with guided suggestions as they internalized their skills to ac-complish basic competency, with plentiful feedback from their father.

After the young men became adept at their father's foundational tech-niques, they were skilled enough to fish well. To become a master of his craft, though, Paul Maclean breaks from his father's structured cast and stylizes a version all his own. What started as a structured lesson in fly casting evolved to become an individualized form of expression.

Without recognizing it, the Reverend Maclean was a masterful in-structor. His instruction led from tutored instruction to mastery of skills to individual expression and creativity. Shouldn't that be the goal for any classroom?

In most cases, things people do well are what they learn methodically and practice often. At some point, they internalized their instruction then individualized it, creating some unique technique or distinctive form of expression. The learning process is a delicate one, though. Learning needs to be carefully nurtured. The techniques and strategies described below provide a framework for systematic success with students.

THE POWER OF MODELS

When a high school sophomore was having difficulties in science class, his father scheduled a parent-student-teacher conference. Skimming his son's grade printout, he immediately found the problem: low lab-report scores. His son's science teacher was a friendly educator, popular with his students, knowledgeable in his content. When asked about the lab reports, the teacher produced some of his son's work and could identify that, indeed, this is where he had fallen short.

"How do the students know what a good lab report looks like?" the father inquired. The science teacher leaned from his chair and removed an overhead sheet pinned to his bulletin board. He handed it the father who skimmed it. The report was in a student's handwriting.

"At the beginning of the quarter, I put this 'A-level' lab report on the overhead and talk about it," the science teacher explained. "I leave it on the bulletin board for students who want to refer to it again." At the father's prompting, the teacher made a copy of the report for the man's son.

When the conference resumed, the science teacher led a discussion of the model lab report while the young man labeled in the margins the critical elements identified by the teacher. They spent the rest of the conference comparing the son's lab reports with the model. As they discussed the work, the teen could see where his efforts had fallen short. When the teenager created his next lab report, he had a copy of the model beside him. As the student wrote the next report, he made sure to add the components his teacher thought critical. As a result, the quality of his lab reports improved immediately, as did his grade in the class.

Students want to be successful. Often, though, they don't know precisely what success looks like. Teachers give them instructions and tell them what to do, and then students often go about blindly groping for a product that would meet the concept of success.

Educators, though, can help out students greatly by showing them what success looks like. Examples of exemplary paragraphs, essays, lab reports, final projects, etc., are called models. Concrete models of successful work or projects can be that essential element that guides student growth and effort.

From lab reports to golf swings, examples of excellence are essential when expecting students to learn some new skill (albeit they are less helpful for conceptual understanding embedded in schematic understanding—science and math concepts, for example). The models also need to be readily available to students.

Models for writing instruction, for example, can be particularly powerful. Writers trying to achieve a certain writing goal do well studying exemplary models before the writing task begins. Take, for example, paragraph writing. If teachers want students to write well-constructed paragraphs, they need to show students examples of excellent writing products appropriate for their grade level.

Models of exemplary work placed under document cameras work well for classroom discussions about strong topic sentences, well-elaborated text-based examples for support, and an effective clincher sentence. Teachers can lead the analysis about how the individual parts function to create a well-explained whole. In the margins, teachers can write notes as the students identify the paragraph's critical elements. Students can mark up their own copies.

When analyzing good selections of writing style, teachers can go a step further. Rather than just discuss exemplary articles, editorials, and book passages, teachers can assign students to either word-process the selections or hand write them to see how they would look had the students written them themselves. In writing, the length of sentences and paragraphs, punctuation, and word choice all contribute to writing style and author's voice.

Close analysis of models written or typed in a format familiar to students gives them a sense of what teachers are looking for. Next, students can compare and contrast the length of their sentences, the syntax, the punctuation, and the word choice with the exemplary selections. Looking at exemplary work "as if you had written it" is a solid method for identifying elements of voice and style. Students learn areas where they can improve and grow.

Teachers can take the analysis of models a step further by providing examples of high- *and* low-quality work for skill development. Asking students to compare and contrast the traits of work samples of varied qualities requires them to deduce what makes student products good and what makes others fall short. Through their digging, they unearth standards of quality.

Discussion about what makes excellent work, what meets course standards, and what may be missing from emerging products is a powerful way to imprint standards of success. When students know what different levels of success look like, they have a target to aim for.

Models can be used throughout our educational system. For example, some state-mandated math tests require students to not only show their work in math but also explain their thinking. Models of success for appropriate elaboration can be critical to bringing students to required standards. Why not show students what a well-explained math problem looks like? Released (archived) items are often available that show varied levels of proficiency.

Models of top-scoring math answers provide solid examples for students of the targets they need to achieve for skill development or procedural work. Examples of work that falls short of excellence prompt students to identify why the models fell short; as a result, they apply this learning to improving their own answers.

Models are powerful in career and technical classes as well. In wood or auto shop, models of excellent finishes, for instance, give students an example of the quality expected of the final project. Examples of a poor finish and the mistakes that produced it are important learning tools. In an orchestra class, students can listen to a professionally produced selection as they work to tackle a selection themselves. With a proper example of excellence, students don't become confused about the final sound.

When completing complex technology projects, models can be essential for helping students get all the elements correct. For example, multimedia projects are an excellent way to synthesize understanding at the end of a unit. (Microsoft Photo Story is a free download and easy to use; video-editing software like Microsoft Movie Maker or Apple iMovie comes loaded on new computers.) Photos, text, narration, and background music can all be combined to create a professional effect.

Teachers either create these exemplars or collect them from past student work. Teachers should also show examples of projects that fell short of standards—this can be an effective way to remind students of all the elements that need to be included. Students should analyze all these models in terms of the final rubric for the project, which should contain descriptors of levels of excellence for all important project categories.

These models for final multimedia projects should contain all the elements required in the final product: the number of photos, appropriate background music, voice-overs, and text. Students review and analyze these examples. Therefore, before the students begin their projects, they know what the outcome of their efforts should be.

These models inform students about the depth of content required for a quality project. Models provide students the standards they need to meet when completing their projects—a vital component to establishing excellence in classrooms.

Of course, models should be just that: guides. Students should be given broad latitude to meet the desired outcomes in an individualized way. While lessons can become less effective without models, damage can also be done when students think a model is a strict guideline.

Never should models be used to stifle creativity or innovation—they should only be used to provide direction. It would be foolish, for example, to think that a great paragraph should contain the same number of sentences as the model paragraph, yet teachers sometimes fall into this trap. One of the great mistakes writing teachers can make is to overemphasize structured formulas. An extremely rigid formula for expository essays can dictate the number and style of sentences in paragraphs, including predictable transitions such as "first," "second," or "third," to introduce examples.

While easy to teach and easy to learn, stiff formulas lead to rigid, dull writing—a challenge for the next teacher who has to loosen up writers taught to write in an overly prescriptive, uncreative way.

Models may be the single most potent strategy for moving students' skills to standards of excellence. Models need to be guides to point students in the right direction—but not be rigid formulas. Analyzing the differences between excellent and less-than-satisfactory outcomes gives students the information they need to know to revise their own work. Students should be asked to exceed the model's standards whenever possible.

The Reflective Teacher

- What concrete models of excellence do I provide my students as targets before they begin a new task?

COMMUNICATE LEARNING TARGETS: RUBRICS

Most likely, anyone who has a decade or more of teaching experience has at some time scrawled a fraction across the top of an assignment to communicate a grade. A 93/100, for example, might communicate that the paper was in the 90 percent or above range and worthy of an A. Perhaps an "Excellent job" or similar comment was scrawled across the assignment, as well. Based on fairly sophisticated thinking, the teacher concluded that the work was excellent. Likewise, assignments that reflect less quality received lower percentages and lower grades.

Unless teachers are dealing with a specific fact or solution (something quantitative), assessment is to some degree subjective. One teacher might give an assignment a "93 percent," while another might have awarded the work an "89 percent"; another teacher might have felt a "97 percent" was appropriate.

A reasonable variation is to be expected; teachers are humans dealing with qualitative topics. The harm of the ambiguity of assessment, though, lies not in the assigning of a specific grade. The damage lies when the grade or comments given fail to communicate to students, with a reasonable degree of specificity, how they performed and what they might do to improve on future attempts.

One way to establish clear understanding between students and the standards teachers expect of them is through rubrics. A rubric is a list or a table of descriptors that quantify different levels of success. The descriptors attempt to quantify the critical qualities found in the models given to students.

While models are indispensable tools for giving tangible examples of learning targets, quality rubrics are key to communicating learning standards. The careful selection of criteria about what constitutes a 4, 3, 2, or 1 on a four-point rubric (with 4 being the top score), for example, removes much of the ambiguity of assessment and gives the student key information for improvement.

Rubrics, when used with models, provide tangible learning targets for students. By providing a fixed, understandable target, students have something to aim for. A big reason students may fall short in their performance is that they may not know what constitutes excellence.

By providing models and rubrics, then thoroughly exploring how the rubric defines excellence in the model, teachers give students concrete definitions and examples of success. When teachers assess and assign scores using a rubric, the number given communicates what a score means based on tangible criteria. Through rubrics, teachers communicate to students where they excelled and where they fell short.

While many rubrics are based on a four-point scale, some are based on different scales. Some holistic rubrics, for example, use a nine-point scale. Other rubrics use three-point scales. Four-point rubrics are probably the most common. They are broken out to define the following:

- Exceeds standard (the highest scores — 4 on a four-point rubric)
- Meets standard (a 3 on a four-point rubric)

- Approaching but not yet achieving standard (a 2 on a four-point rubric)
- Emerging (a 1 on a four-point rubric)

Rubrics can come in two forms: analytic and holistic. For many state-level assessments, students are evaluated using a holistic rubric, largely for expediency's sake. The holistic rubric gives descriptors for key traits, but all the descriptors for 4s, for example, are lumped together. The entire test answer, assignment, or project is given only one holistic score. See the following paragraph-writing holistic rubric.

Score of 4

- Topic sentence answers the prompt in precise language (title and/or author are added).
- At least two examples of well-elaborated, text-based evidence are used.
- All elements of the student work precisely support the topic sentence.
- Concludes with a clincher sentence that relates tightly to the topic sentence.
- Sentences or phrases of varied length and structure create a purposeful sense of rhythm and voice.
- Uses language effectively by exhibiting choices that are engaging and appropriate for intended audience and purpose.

Score of 3

- Topic sentence answers the prompt in general language (title and/or author are added).
- At least one example of well-elaborated, text-based evidence is used.
- All elements of the student work generally support the topic sentence.
- Concludes with a clincher sentence that relates to the topic sentence.
- Includes sentences or phrases where appropriate of varied length and structure.

- Uses adequate language and appropriate word choices for intended audience and purpose.

Score of 2

- Topic sentence somewhat answers the prompt.
- An example(s) is used but it is not well elaborated.
- Some (but not all) elements of student work support the topic sentence.
- Clincher sentence does not closely relate to the topic sentence.
- Includes mostly simple sentences throughout; attempt at variety in structure.
- Has a limited and predictable vocabulary that may not be appropriate for the intended audience and purpose.

Score of 1

- Topic sentence does not relate to the prompt.
- No examples are given or, if given, do not support the topic sentence.
- Few elements support the topic sentence.
- Does not conclude with a clincher sentence.
- Simple sentences; some incomplete sentences.
- Has a limited or inappropriate vocabulary for the intended audience and purpose.

While holistic rubrics remove much of the ambiguity of how scores are derived, the analytic rubric, which allows teachers to assess the quality of key individual traits (organized into tables), is a more precise tool at the classroom level to communicate to students where they stand on a variety of important skills. (See Table 3.1 for a paragraph writing analytic rubric.)

For example, a student in writing may perform well in ideas and organization and deserve a 4 but may underperform in word choice and sentence fluency and receives a 2. Using a holistic rubric, the teacher or assessor, seeing that some parts of the writing are a 4 and some a 2, might assign a 3 to the writing project to average the difference.

Using an analytic rubric, though, scores of 4s may be assigned to ideas and organization while word choice and sentence fluency get 2s.

Table 3.1. Expository Paragraph Analytic Writing Rubric (Based on College Board Standards W2.2, W3.1, W3.2, W4.1, W5.1, and W5.4)

CRITERIA	4	3	2	1
Topic Sentence	• Topic sentence answers the prompt in precise language. (Title and/or author are added.)	• Topic sentence answers the prompt in general language. (Title and/or author are added.)	• Topic sentence sort of answers the prompt.	• Topic sentence does not relate to the prompt.
Ideas	• At least two examples of well-elaborated text-based evidence are used.	• At least one example of well-elaborated text-based evidence is used.	• An example(s) is used but it is not well elaborated.	• No examples are given or, if given, do not support the topic sentence.
Coherence of Ideas	• All elements of the student work precisely support the topic sentence.	• All elements of the student work generally support the topic sentence.	• Some elements (but not all) of student work support the topic sentence.	• Few elements support the topic sentence.
Clincher Sentence	• Concludes with a clincher sentence that relates tightly to the topic sentence.	• Concludes with a clincher sentence that relates to the topic sentence.	• Clincher sentence does not closely relate to the topic sentence.	• Does not conclude with a clincher sentence.
Syntax (Sentence Fluency)	• Sentences or phrases of varied length and structure create a purposeful sense of rhythm and voice.	• Includes sentences or phrases, where appropriate, of varied length and structure.	• Includes mostly simple sentences throughout; attempt at variety in structure.	• Simple sentences; some incomplete sentences.
Diction (Word Choice)	• Uses language effectively by exhibiting choices that are engaging and appropriate for intended audience and purpose.	• Uses adequate language and appropriate word choices for intended audience and purpose.	• Has a limited and predictable vocabulary which may not be appropriate for the intended audience and purpose.	• Has a limited or inappropriate vocabulary for the intended audience and purpose.

From the student's perspective, he or she knows that extra energy needs to be directed toward word choice and sentence fluency. This level of communication provides precise feedback for classroom use.

Holistic rubrics may be a necessity for assessing large quantities of summative assignments (such as state-mandated tests). Due to their less prescriptive nature, though, holistic rubrics may not be the best classroom tool to communicate areas where students need to grow. The same rubric may be used over a variety of grade levels. Its interpretation, though, will vary based on standards of expected performance at each grade level.

Internalizing rubrics becomes a key to student success, especially if teachers are working on life-long skills like writing. For example, a 4 in Ideas on a writing rubric may read, "Maintains consistent focus on topic and has selected relevant details." Whether the writer is a high school student working to pass a state-mandated test for graduation, a feature-story freelancer for a major magazine, or an angry middle-aged citizen composing a letter to the editor, this standard for top score in "Ideas" applies; its interpretation just changes due to the length and sophistication of the project.

Carefully selected models and rubrics, when studied, applied, and revisited again and again, create a permanent inner landscape in students that guides them when they are beyond the schoolhouse doors.

Rubrics can be a vital tool to communicating the standards for complex projects. For example, Washington State Constitutional Issues Classroom Based Assessment (CBA) recommended for eighth grade is a complex performance task that can take weeks to complete properly. The project requires that students research constitutional topics and the conflicts they create, then present their opinions in an extended-response persuasive essay based on the stance they took on a constitution issue.[1]

This CBA is an excellent example of an overarching summative assessment meant to synthesize a variety of content knowledge and writing skills. The descriptors for a 4 are as follows. Students take a position on the issue that:

- Considers both individual rights and the common good.
- Includes a call to action.

They provide background on the issue by describing:

- What the issue is.
- Who is involved in the issue.
- Why this issue is important, by relating it to a key ideal or constitutional principle.

They provide reason(s) for the position supported by evidence. The evidence:

- Includes an explanation of how a constitutional principle logically supports the position on the issue.
- Includes an explanation of how two or more additional pieces of credible information logically support the position on the issue.
- Makes explicit references to four or more credible sources that provide relevant information.
- Cites sources within the paper, presentation, or bibliography.

Before students begin the research for the CBA, they are given the rubric so they know upfront what is expected in their final project. As they collect research information, consider democratic ideals and constitution principles, and seek to find a balance between individual rights and the common good, they know the standards for success. As teachers assess student progress *during* the project, they can give formative feedback based on the CBA rubric. The rubric provides a common language for discussion.

By clarifying the expectations stated in the rubric by comparing the intent of the descriptors with student work, teachers keep students progressing and on target.

When using a rubric for assessment, teachers checking boxes and underlining key wording in descriptors helps to communicate ideas clearly to students. Converting a rubric score to a grade can be a bit tricky since some parts of the rubric may have more value than others.

One solution is to give a greater weighting to more important elements of the rubric. With a multimedia project, for example, a teacher may want the category of Content to be weighted more heavily than categories like Project Length, Images, or Sound Track (see Table 3.2). Without

Table 3.2. Multimedia-Presentation Analytic Rubric

CRITERIA	4	3	2	1
Content (Multiplied by 3)	Presentation clearly identifies a problem and offers a clear solution to it.	Presentation identifies the problem and offers a solution to it.	In the presentation, the problem or a solution are not clearly tied to the topic.	Presentation does not clearly identify a problem or solution.
Project Length	Presentation is approximately 60 seconds in length.	Presentation is close to 60 seconds in length.	Presentation is either way under 60 seconds or way over 60 seconds.	Presentation is only partially complete or unedited to length.
Images	Images are high quality and support the theme of the project.	Images are adequate and seem to support the theme.	Images are not quite adequate or may not support the theme.	An attempt was made at adding relevant images.
Soundtrack– Music Selection	Music stirs a rich, emotional response that matches the story line well. Music does not intrude upon the narration.	Music stirs a response that supports the story line. Music does not intrude upon the narration.	Music may somewhat detract from the story line. Music may intrude upon the narration.	Music detracts from the story line. Music intrudes upon the narration.
Soundtrack – Student Voice Track	The narration is very appropriate for the tone of the project. Narrators speak clearly.	The narration is appropriate for the tone of the project. Narrators are understandable.	The narration may not be appropriate for the tone of the project. Narrators are not always understandable.	The narration is not appropriate for the tone of the project. Narrators are not understandable.
Participation	All members participated equally in the project.	All members participated in the project.	The presentation was produced by a few members.	One person largely did the project.
Works Cited	Three relevant sources are found in the Works Cited. Sources are properly cited.	Two relevant sources are found in the Works Cited. Sources are properly cited.	One relevant source is found in the Works Cited.	No Works Cited was added to the presentation.

relevant, quality content, multimedia presentations won't convey much meaning. Teachers might multiply the Content scores by 3 and leave the remaining traits at their standard value to emphasize its importance.

While rubrics are a powerful tools for students, creating one collaboratively with a group of fellow teachers or a department can go a long way toward clarifying the expectations for a common test, project, or assignment. Online programs like RubiStar are a good way to create a rough draft.[2]

The collective discussion about the precise language for the rubric descriptors can lead to an important "meeting of the minds" about the intent of the project and what a successful outcome really looks like. When a group of teachers can agree on the descriptors of a rubric, they typically understand the scope of the project and the expectations for students.

Typically, despite teachers' best efforts, rubrics need to be tweaked after a project has been completed to align its wording with the expectations for the project. Rarely is a rubric perfect the first time around. Often, students' interpretation when reading a rubric will vary from the teachers' intention, and revision is needed to make the descriptors more accurate and understandable. This is to be expected as part of the lesson or project-revision process.

Rubrics are essential for communicating standards of success. The creation of rubrics demands that teachers identify precisely their expectation for student learning.

Used together, models and rubrics give students precise targets for academic success.

The Reflective Teacher

- How do I communicate my standards for success to my students?

CREATING STEPS TO SUCCESS: SCAFFOLD LEARNING

For meaningful growth to take place, a gap exists between where students are in their knowledge and skills when they enter a grade level, course, or unit, and the standards they need to achieve. In a given classroom, students arrive with a variety of knowledge and skill levels. Add to that the fact that they progress at different rates.

If teaching to this array of abilities appears to be a daunting task, it is. The job of educators, though, is to move students, no matter their level, forward along the standards continuum, a concept called "value added." To accomplish this, teaching needs to be a thoughtful, intentional process for knowledge and skill building, one offering plenty of support to students.

The challenge for teachers is how to move students forward. Models and rubrics are essential. They give concrete examples of the destination for student growth. But how do teachers go about actually boosting the students' skills to a level whereby they meet, and hopefully exceed, course standards?

Key to student success is thoughtfully designed lessons, organizers, and checkpoints that make "thinking visible." A succession of activities and the graphic organizers, checklists, and templates that make a thoughtful process unfold visibly is often lumped under the term "scaffolding." Like the scaffolds used on constructions sites, these organizers of thinking, analysis, and synthesis are crucial to the creation of a thoughtful, logical mental landscape that prepares students to perform complex tasks long after they have left the classroom.

Like models of success, scaffolding is not meant to constrict student creativity. Scaffolds are designed to give students a model for thinking, knowing that teachers will allow flexibility if an effective, alternative process works better for the students. Scaffolds have limited use when creating conceptual understanding in areas like math and science, but for skill building and methodical-thinking practices, they can be indispensable.

When teachers create scaffolds, they are modeling the metacognitive processes that are needed to be successful for the required task. The process for the scaffolding learning goes as follows:

- Teachers create the first scaffolds (organizational tools and processes) for students to use.
- Students use the scaffolding provided by their teacher, modifying it if necessary to fit their own needs. Students internalize and mimic the organization or thinking process.
- After internalizing the organizational or thinking techniques, students apply their own versions of these processes as they become independent learners.

Take, for example, teaching compare-and-contrast skills in a science unit. To scaffold student thinking, the science teacher assigns the use of a Venn diagram to direct students to list the similarities and differences between cell processes such as photosynthesis and respiration. This graphic organizer makes student thinking visible, which allows the teacher to assess students' cognitive processes. Based on the degree of elaboration in the diagram, the teacher may direct students to look more closely at traits that may have been misunderstood or overlooked. The instructor may ask probing questions to direct students toward deeper understanding or to redirect incorrect thinking. A well-populated Venn diagram becomes evidence of careful observation and compare-contrast thinking.

Since a goal of this scaffold is to internalize compare-contrast thinking strategies, the students carry away from the task the analysis skills prompted by the Venn diagram. Later in life, when students as adults are comparing and contrasting features of cars, televisions, or homes, they might create some document to help them with their thinking. It could be a list. It could be a diagram of sorts. Most likely, a Venn diagram itself probably wouldn't be used, but the thinking patterns that it at one time fostered would be. Nonetheless, the structured pattern of comparing and contrasting from the use of a Venn diagram in school carries over into an individualized thinking structure used in later life.

Sometimes, educators do a disservice to their students by assuming they have the thinking skills necessary to complete tasks of analysis, synthesis, or observation. Teachers should carefully structure the activity with appropriate scaffolding to make student thinking visible. Students who are falling short in the necessary skills can be pulled aside and helped in small groups.

Modeling a methodical thinking process is as important as any skills educators teach. Scaffolding the learning process with careful structure and support material is a solid way to build thinking patterns.

The most common form of scaffolding is graphic organizers. For years, English teachers have used T-charts to help students analyze the literature they are reading. In the left-hand column, the English students write a passage that would pique their interest, while in the right-hand column they respond to the passage with some specific forms of literary analysis.

Basically, what these teachers were doing for their students was prompting them to analyze literature in a prescribed way (stage one of scaffolding). As important, though, teachers are giving themselves a tool to assess student understanding and a platform to assist students in correcting their thinking. The ultimate goal is to make students independent thinkers in their analysis of the books they read or the movies they see. Only lined paper is needed for this task.

Venn diagrams, KWL charts (what you Know, what you Want to know, and what you have Learned), literary plot triangles, and a variety of graphics organizers are easily created on computers, saved as document templates, and ready for student use in electronic form or as pencil-and-paper tasks, whichever is more appropriate at the time.

Another form of scaffolding that is often overlooked is the checklist. Whether it be a science report or history activity, a checklist of critical parts helps keep students on target as they create a final product or complete a lengthy project. Before the final product is handed to the teacher, a student peer edits the project using the checklist to identify critical elements and ensure they exist. If important components are missing, they can be added before the teacher assesses the project.

When working in a project-based learning environment, a simple checklist is quite valuable for keeping students on track. Many of the tasks that students are completing can get quite complex (Washington State Social Studies Classroom Based Assessments come with extensive checklists). To make sure students achieve success, use checklists to guide them through the project. In adult life, they will use checklists to keep track of daily appointments, groceries that must be purchased, and activities that need to be completed. Students should be trained to use checklists as well. Teachers can scaffold student success through a variety of checklist-style organizers:

Simple Checklist: For longer projects that students need to accomplish, give students a list of the required tasks. As simple as this may seem, checklists keep students on track. Checklists also result in fewer questions being asked of teachers and fewer omissions of critical elements when projects are complete.

Performance Checklist: These checklists are a great way to get students thinking about the quality of their work. A list of numbers follows the items on the checklist: 1 to 4, 1 to 5, or 1 to 10. Rather than a simple list of items to complete, a performance checklist asks students to rate the quality of their performance by circling the numbers of the items to be completed, with the highest numbers representing excellent quality. Performance checklists serve like a simplified rubric; they just lack the in-depth descriptors.

Templates: These are the next step up from a checklist. A template prompts students to add specific elements to achieve a requested format. When students are learning to write a letter to the editor, for example, a template is a useful way to guide their learning. Reminders of what each paragraph of text should contain helps students structure their writing.

Again, scaffolds like these provide structure for students new to the process. As students become more proficient, they depart from the suggested organizational structure and write in a more individualized style. A lab report could be scaffolded in a similar fashion. See the following persuasive-letter template:

Place date here: Month, date, and year (Example: March 14, 2011)

Writer's name
Writer's street address
Writer's city, state, zip code

The person to whom the letter is to be sent
Name of company or government committee or building
Address
City, state, zip code

Dear (Recipient of the letter, include title):

Write your introductory paragraph here. The purpose of the introductory paragraph is to hook reader interest and state the point of your letter (your thesis). Keep your intro paragraph succinct.

Write your first body paragraph here. The purpose of all body paragraphs is to use facts and examples to explain the point of your letter. Remember, you must stick to the point stated in your thesis. In this first body paragraph, though, you must add a concession. This is best done at the top or near the top of your body paragraph. Remember, to follow your concession with an argument that pulls your reader back to your side. Write with conviction!

Write the remainder of your body paragraphs here. (Hit enter twice between body paragraphs.) The purpose of all body paragraphs is to use facts and examples to explain the point of your letter. Remember, you must stick to the point stated in your thesis. Write with conviction!

Write your closing paragraph here. In this paragraph, provide closure for your letter. It is often best to restate your thesis. Finish with an appropriate call to action.

Sincerely,
Sign your name here
Type your name below your signature

Hidden Text Word Scaffolds: These function as templates except they use a feature in Microsoft Word called hidden text, which is a type of font formatting. To create hidden text, teachers highlight the instructions then go to font formatting and check the hidden-text box. When students click on the show/hide button (it looks like a reverse paragraph symbol in the tool bar), the template instructions disappear and the work looks like regular draft. Word's hidden-text feature can be a powerful electronic tool to scaffold learning.

Hidden Slides in PowerPoint: This concept is the same as hidden text except that rather than hide text, teachers hide the slides. These PowerPoint slides are visible when students work on their projects but do not appear when the software is in presentation mode. To create a hidden slide, PowerPoint must be in normal view. Next, left click on the desired slide, right click, and choose Hide Slide from the options. A slash will appear across the slide number in the margin left of the slide. To unhide a slide, reverse the process. Teachers using PowerPoint as a student presentation tool can place instructions on hidden slides for the student slides that are to follow. Since PowerPoint is designed to be visual support for an oral presentation, hidden slides can be a very effective means of scaffolding critical organizational skills.

PowerPoint Portfolio: This functions like a checklist but can be much more effective. Rather than explaining a project orally and giving students a written description of the task, teachers can create a PowerPoint presentation, with different slides showing the varied aspects of the task. In the PowerPoint instructions, teachers can list the tasks to be completed. Using hyperlinks, teachers can direct students to regular checklists, performance checklists, models of final projects, necessary rubrics, and important websites. Students can then access the presentation online or through a network. Certainly this same thing can be accomplished with reams of paper, but PowerPoint is more efficient and easier to update with revisions and a more powerful way to keep students organized.

Essentially, scaffolding, in many instances, is another form of model. Graphic organizers model the thinking process; they make thinking visible so teachers can see where a student succeeds or needs assistance. Checklists model an organizational process. Templates model structures as well.

Scaffolding, as its metaphorical origin suggests, is a temporary process teachers place upon students. It is meant to support a specific task—then it is removed. Like a building, a student should be self-reliant after scaffolding's removal. Scaffolding is meant to be temporary, not a rigid guideline. Used properly, though, scaffolds create the steps that lead students toward meeting and exceeding the standards displayed in models and rubrics.

The Reflective Teacher

- How do I go about effectively supporting my students' learning in a step-by-step process?

ASSESSMENT FOR LEARNING

Imagine a high school football coach on a playing field in late August. He is surrounded by a group of eager players. As a part of their first practice, the football coach makes sure his expectations are clear. Players are expected to learn their positions based on the football manual to be distributed. Each player will be evaluated daily by coaches watching from the sidelines.

At the end of each practice, players will receive a card with a single score that will evaluate the young players on attitude, hustle, *and* skill level. Most comments will be written; very little feedback will be given orally. Game performance will receive higher points. Further, all game and practice scores—from the first day of practice through the end of the season—will be averaged. Only those who hit an 80 percent or higher will be eligible for athletic letters.

One doesn't have to have athletic experience to see the dysfunction of the coaching scenario above. In the movies or in real life, successful coaches, whether they be leading football, basketball, or other teams, are deeply involved with the players, standing among them while they practice, regularly assessing progress, continually making suggestions, constantly encouraging better performance. The coaches' goal is to prepare their players for game day, an authentic performance task where everything taught will be put to the test.

As odd as the "imagined" coaching situation above may sound, many classrooms function like the dysfunctional football scenario described. Performance is assessed daily if class work is graded, and it impacts the final grade; little or no penalty-free practice exists. All grades are averaged. When grades are given for daily work, they may be accompanied with little or no feedback to the student.

Perhaps this method of teaching without abundant feedback explains why some students who underperform in the classroom excel under proficient coaches on the playing field or the court. Regular feedback and encouragement breed success.

A common attribute of great coaches and excellent teachers is the fine-tuned feedback directed at skill building. Few speak as passionately about the need for focused skill-building feedback as assessment guru Rick Stiggins. In his books, lectures, articles, and workshops, Stiggins drives a cleaver through assessment practices, chopping them into two very distinctive parts: "assessment *of* learning" and "assessment *for* learning."[3]

Assessment *of* learning is summative assessment, a "post mortem attempt" as Stiggins puts it, designed to gauge the level of learning that has taken place. These assessment practices include final tests, final papers, final projects, and government-mandated standardized tests. The purpose of these tests is to evaluate student learning *after* the learning process takes place.

While information gathered from these tests may be used to inform future work, assessment of learning is largely the final measuring stick for the student. In most instances, teachers move on to the next unit after the summative assessment. Assessment of learning represents the measure of the growth that has taken place by the end—a process not too different from the farmer taking a tape measure to gauge the final height of his corn.

The power to change student learning dramatically, though, lies not in summative evaluation (which ironically is such an emphasis at the administrative and government level) but in formative assessment, assessment *for* learning. Perhaps it may seem odd that teachers even need to discuss such a simple topic. Of course the purpose of the teaching is to help students build the skills necessary to meet learning targets. Unfortunately, in many classrooms, this is not the case. What Stiggins has found through research is that the culture in classrooms subtly undermines the learning process for many of our students. In the race to meet curriculum timelines, teachers fail to give students the in-depth descriptive feedback (assessment for learning) they really need. Oftentimes, grading efforts discourage students and kill initiative.

Emphasizing assessment for learning places the teacher in the role similar to an effective coach. Like a coach who tries to create a bridge between a player's current level of skills and where he or she needs to grow to perform more effectively, the teacher focuses on diagnosing the spread between each student's current skill level or conceptual understanding and the standards he or she needs to meet; the teacher next prescribes steps to close that gap.

Initially in the process, the teacher prescribes the steps for growth. When this process is in full bloom, though, students become assessors of their own progress and team with the teacher to plan the steps necessary to grow and meet learning targets (self-assessment). For this process to work, clear learning targets in the forms of standards, rubrics, and models need to be in place to assure that outcomes are clear to both teachers and students. Scaffolds need to support pathways to guide students through the steps of growth. When these are in place, the teacher's daily role is to nurture student learning through assessment for learning.

The learning process of a classroom rich in feedback sounds so simple and logical. Yet these rich, supportive learning environments are a challenge to create due to time constraints and lack of knowledge about how to do it. Teachers become adept at assigning reading, lecturing to classes, demonstrating skills, engaging students in discovery lessons, and presenting targets.

So far so good. The teacher has taught the material and the student has practiced it. What is a challenge to create, though, is a personalized strategy for growth for each student. Too often the activity ends only with a grade—when instead each assignment rich in feedback should be a step leading to the next level of skills or understanding.

Many parents have seen firsthand the lack of detailed feedback in schoolwork returned to their children. Student assignments are returned with grades and some positive comments—but very little specific written instruction on what steps should be taken for improvement. These teachers and professors may be highly regarded. They just provide little or no descriptive feedback.

Two elements in implementing "assessment *for* learning" are time and precise, effective feedback that fosters growth. Teachers in general are pinched for time in their content areas. Whether working with semesters or trimesters, class time is often a rush to get everything required "covered" on time. Providing quality descriptive feedback—the kind that really promotes student thinking and growth—takes time, however. Basically, teachers need to find time to prescribe descriptive feedback and communicate it to students (the most effective being one on one); students need time to self-assess their own skills and reflect on ways to improve them.

The solution lies in setting priorities. Something of less importance needs to go by the wayside. In his *The Seven Habits of Highly Effective People*, motivational writer and speaker Stephen Covey talks of "putting first things first." Covey defines those "first things" not as those brush fires that distract people.[4] Instead, "first things" are matters of less-pressing immediate importance that, if attended to now, pay big dividends down the road.

Teachers consistently deal with these "brush fires": the disruptions, the discipline issues, the completing of required assessments on time. All need to be taken care of because they are pressing. Yet if the purpose of educators is to make students better scientists, mathematicians, readers, writers, thinkers, etc., a critical task is to provide them with abundant, quality feedback to accomplish these skills. And this feedback needs to be given plentifully and regularly.

Prioritizing instruction is a challenge every classroom teacher faces. The first steps in assessment for learning is determining what is most important in a classroom then managing class time and/or activities to accomplish it. Some activities of less importance may need to be dropped.

At other times, though, teachers can differentiate instruction by pulling together into groups students experiencing the same deficits in their skills or conceptual understanding. The teacher can work with these smaller groups of students while the rest of the class continues on with other activities. The logistics of accomplishing this form of differentiation will be discussed more in the next chapter.

The second step in implementing assessment for learning may be the most challenging: providing pinpoint, effective feedback (or questions) that moves students to the necessary understanding of the skill or concept to be mastered. This precise feedback—called "descriptive feedback" due to its illuminating nature—could come in the form of suggestions, but teachers may also guide students to the necessary understanding through a series of carefully crafted questions. Descriptive feedback or guided questioning empowers students to bridge the gap between where they are in their skill level or conceptual understanding and where they need to be.

This growth-building descriptive feedback can come in the form of written commentary on papers or activities. This typically is the most common way teachers communicate feedback to their students. It takes time to read the student work, time to write commentary, and time to explain any misunderstandings that students may have about the commentary. Pinpoint feedback or thought-provoking questions, though, can produce marvellous results in student growth.

Conversation and dialogue, though less formal, can be just as effective, but they have additional benefits. To accomplish this, teachers circulate among their students as they are working on the assigned activity, answering their questions or making suggestions while informally assessing their work. Descriptive feedback or guided questioning during the activity can immediately remedy mistakes students may be making, possibly reducing or even eliminating the need for commentary later.

Perhaps more important, though, is the impact this personal attention has upon students. When teachers work with students one on one, they affirm them as people. These teachers show students that they are valued as thinkers, learners, and individuals. These teachers show students that *their thinking matters*.

To provide effective descriptive feedback, teachers need to have a thorough grasp of the content area being taught and an understanding of how students, step by step, typically go about learning it. This content knowledge comes from a solid understanding of the subject matter or skills being taught.

Knowing where students stumble and struggle must become an integral part of the teacher's knowledge base. Collaborative discussions between teachers, though, can lessen this learning curve. By looking at student work together (using a formal protocol to direct discussion), experienced teachers can share their insights and understanding with newer teachers. All can share the type of challenges they face and the solutions that work; innovative ideas often come from those new to the field as well. Through this process, teachers can build the bank of understanding required for giving effective feedback to students.

Feedback needs to be effectively shaped to be valuable. For feedback to be effective, Stiggins states, it must be "descriptive" not evaluative.[5] Anyone who has worked to improve the quality of feedback to their students can attest to how challenging this can be. Evaluative feedback means placing judgment on the work the student has completed. For example, placing a grade of 7/10 on an assignment then adding "good job" (or a similar upbeat phrase) to make the student feel better is evaluative feedback.

While most teachers may see this comment as a pat on the back for students, Stiggins contends that comments like this might do the opposite. The teacher giving a C on the assignment plus a comment of "good job" may stifle future initiative—the translation being that a student's best effort results in only a passing grade. Further, the grade and comment transmit no feedback that tells the student what growth needs to take place to move from a C to a better grade.

Additionally, less-than-perfect grades on practice work can stifle risk taking. Like the football players described above, grading each practice reduces the freedom students have for "penalty free" practice. Grading every assignment has the potential to stifle risk taking. Few adults want to try anything that makes them look bad; students think the same way. Therefore, Stiggins recommends that all practice work receive no grades so that students focus on growth rather than the grade they will be receiving.[6]

If some sort of mark needs to be given, this author suggests that teachers consider giving credit of some form to honor the effort taken

At the core of this movement, though, is a deep shift in priorities. The shift is away from grading largely on process and work ethic, toward grading based on acquired skills, content knowledge, and conceptual understanding.

One of the biggest challenges of the standards-based teaching movement is persuading teachers of the necessity of basing their grades on the level of mastery of learning targets and standards rather than largely on effort. When copious points are doled out for assignments completed (or not given due to missing work), the results can heavily skew a grade. Essentially, points are given as a reward for students completing their work in a given quality and a timely fashion. The learning process—as opposed to learning outcomes—is rewarded (or reprimanded, if work is missing).

The movement to change grading practices toward basing grades on skills, content knowledge, and/or conceptual understanding has nothing to do with overtly attempting to diminish students' work habits. A strong work ethic is a critical element for success in achieving good scores in a standards-driven classroom. The goal of standards-based grading is to distill scores down to a meaningful grade that faithfully represents the students' skill levels, content knowledge, and conceptual understanding.

When scores of all kinds—daily work, formative assessments, and summative assessments—are lumped together and then calculated against a percentage, it is sometimes called "grade pollution." For example, what really constitutes an A in a classroom? Is this A a straight calculation of skills that places students at the top of performance on rubrics and grading standards? Or is an A the result of turning in all daily work, which, when calculated together, can create a larger sum in the grade book than the scores from final tests and projects, thus tipping an average grade of C+ on assessments (which may be an accurate evaluation of course skill levels and conceptual understanding) to an A, due to student homework scores?

To further complicate what a grade means, teachers may also factor in "extra-credit" points for activities that have nothing to do with the curriculum. Teachers may give points for participation in school canned-food drives and extra credit if their students return their allotted bathroom passes unused at the end of the grading period. Students can get extra points for turning in additional reports. Such rewards are not uncommon in classrooms. They are incentives to do the proper thing, like tax credits.

Few advocates of standards-based grading, though, would challenge providing students with additional opportunities to revise critical work and raise their competence, but shouldn't a grade have a direct correlation to a student's level of competency in the unit of study?

Grades themselves need to be based on clear standards (communicated clearly, often through rubrics, models, etc.). If teachers are to encourage students toward penalty-free practice, the reward will be the high skill levels they achieve through their work ethic. Typically, the more effort that goes toward building skills and understanding, the better the summative assessment outcome. The students get better scores, they become encouraged, and they work harder. (How many people actually work hard when discouraged?) Rather than focusing on extra-credit make-up assignments, students pour their energies into meeting the learning targets for the class. Again, work habits are of vital importance.

Effort can and should be acknowledged, however. School districts around the country are creating a separate category for work habits on the report card sent to parents. The academic grade reflects academic competence. A separate effort grade reflects work habits. Both growth and work habits are acknowledged. Systems like this also allow teachers to positively reward student effort.

Finally, if teachers assign final grades for quarters, trimesters, or semesters, based on students' best efforts (the skill level they finally achieve, as opposed to averaging high against low scores), students have an incentive to grow without being dragged down by previous performances. Many experienced teachers average grades between quarters to create a semester grade. Others keep a running total for a semester or trimester. Either method discourages student growth if scores for the starting work and ending work for a given skill or concept are averaged.

This question exists, though: Why should a student's final grade be dragged down by poorer early performance if the student can clearly show that he or she has grown to a higher level of competency? If, for example, a student is able to master a given skill or finally understands and can articulate a critical concept before the grading period ends, should that not be factored into the student's final grade—overriding any previous assessment?

Specifically, if a literacy student, for example, struggles with the concept of theme as assessed in unit one, should that grade remain fixed if the student becomes adept at articulating themes later in the grading period?

Unconvinced? Think about grading this way. Say a college student takes a golf class and shoots an 88 for nine holes the first time on the course. Diligent in her practice, this student knocks down her score to the mid-70s then finally shoots a 57 and a 58 on her two final rounds of the semester. Should her final grade for the class reflect an averaging of all scores, the 50s through the high 80s, or should the course grade reflect her best efforts, scores of 57 and 58? The obvious answer is grades should be based on the final scores. Why should it be different in a classroom?

When teachers create grading systems that reward students for their best efforts, they create optimism in the classroom, since students feel they can control their destiny. Rather than the students saying, "What's it matter how hard I try now, I started with a D anyway," they become energized to do better, knowing that the best outcome—which they determine largely through their own effort—will be their reward.

Again, this emphasis on standards-based grading can never come to fruition without the models, rubrics, and other standards that define success. The effort likewise is in vain unless students receive plentiful assessment for learning—the kind that directs them specifically in how they need to grow and can help students answer this question: "Where am I now, and what do I need to do to increase my understanding and skills?"

If teachers are to really nurture student learning, the system of instruction from the first day of class to the end of the grading period should quantify academic progress. Mixing all kinds of effort into a confusing concoction is not the answer.

Teachers nurture student learning by keeping the focus on their standards for students and creating grading systems that give students the information they need to improve. Hard work should pay off—in a quantifiable, interpretable grade.

The Reflective Teacher

- How closely do my scoring practices align student grades to my standards for success?
- To what degree do my grading practices create optimism in my students?

ENCOURAGE SUCCESS

Even with rubrics, appropriate scaffolds, and grading systems that reflect learning growth, some students will either be reluctant to try in class or fall short in their efforts and become discouraged. Sometimes the difference between frustrated students and those swelled by success is the encouragement teachers give to get them to surmount difficult challenges and achieve success. As the saying goes, "Success breeds success"—but students need to build momentum in that direction.

Teachers possess tremendous power to shape student lives for the better. The learning process can be a very fragile thing, though. Learning easy material or skills is a breeze for most anyone, student or adult. However, learning anything challenging is a delicate process, a series of stepping stones that leads down the path to mastery of skills or understanding.

Few students have enough life experience to know that diligence leads to success. They need to learn that success is achieved by continuous steps forward, although some may appear small. Before students can learn to fly, they need to learn to stand and walk and run and climb and dance. By encouraging students, teachers move them toward success and learning this all-so-important life lesson.

CLOSING

If teachers expect students to grow, then they need to make it a conscious practice to nurture student learning. When students understand standards for success, when they receive individualized descriptive feedback, when they are encouraged to take that next step in the learning process, this is when they grow and when student learning flourishes.

Construct Meaning

Writing has essential parts. Whether it's a novel, a feature story, a news story, or an essay, the purpose of the opening of a written selection is to hook reader interest and introduce the guiding idea. The middle is meant to enrich reader understanding through exploring ideas or narrating a series of events. The closing, to be effective, must tie up the writing so that the reader either feels closure or a desire to act. For a written work to be effective, each element must be carefully crafted to achieve the desired impact.

Like the parts of writing, effective lessons or units have stages as well. The teacher's skill at crafting and delivering each element of the lesson will determine whether or not the lesson is engaging and successful.

While our standardized tests and analysis of student data reduces parts of education to a science, teaching is still very much a performance art. Lessons and units, to be effective, must be carefully crafted to achieve the necessary outcomes (meeting a standard or understanding). Effective lessons are crafted using the following distinct parts:

Activate, Engage, and Assess: Student interest is hooked, prior learning and knowledge are engaged, and background knowledge/ necessary skills are assessed and, if necessary, supplemented. Teachers check for naive preconceptions. (Note: The term "naive preconceptions" is used in this chapter rather than the more commonly used term "incorrect preconceptions." In general, people make meaning out of what they see. The term "naive" implies lacking experience, as opposed to "incorrect," which suggests a lack of good-quality thinking.)

Explore, Discover, and Differentiate: A knowledge base is built through exploration and discovery (a constructivist approach), although more didactic methods may be employed. While the exploratory stage is in process, teachers differentiate instruction to assist students individually or in groups.

Synthesize and Integrate: Students synthesize information into a meaningful, relevant final performance task. If applicable, teachers check for the revision of naive preconceptions that may have existed at the start of the lesson.

Reflect and Revise: Teachers assess the effectiveness of the lesson or unit. This may occur while the lesson or unit is in progress and may be in need of redirection. Reflection will also occur at the lesson's end. Teachers use information gathered from final assessments to revise the lesson to make it more effective for future use.

These steps in the teaching process are essential for a successful student-learning experience, and they can be applied to short learning activities or long units.

This chapter is devoted to a deeper understanding of how to Activate, Engage, and Assess; Explore, Discover, and Differentiate; Synthesize and Integrate; and Reflect and Revise each function.

ACTIVATE, ENGAGE, AND ASSESS

For teachers who earned their certificates in the 1980s and 1990s, Madeline Hunter's "Instructional Theory into Practice" (ITIP) was one of education's core philosophies.[1] According to Hunter, each lesson should start with an Anticipatory Set. The purpose of this set was to hook student interest, to get them "ready, set to go."

In other words, teachers didn't start their students immediately working on content. They enticed students to dig into a new lesson by starting with some engaging activity that related to the day's learning objective(s). If continuing a multiday unit, teachers might begin their instruction each day by engaging students in part of what they covered in the last lesson.

Hunter's Anticipatory Set was a great addition to lesson design. While talented teachers applied this concept naturally, for those new to the field, the Anticipatory Set was a reminder that teachers needed to engage students if lessons were to be successful. Still, while innovative, something was missing from Hunter's opening formula. Teachers could hook student interest, but as lessons advanced, not all students were progressing at close to the same rate—even though all were given the same material. Educators know that one reason kids learn at different rates is their natural talents and interests for the subject matter. Still, not all of the variation in student progress could be laid upon these differences.

Research (and common experience) has found that a major factor in student success is the level of background knowledge and necessary skills students bring to the lesson. In some cases, this background knowledge may be personal experience. In other cases, background knowledge may be crucial knowledge or skills learned from the previous unit or year of study. For example, solid background knowledge is critical in world-language and math classes.

If students are not adept at the material from a previous unit or former class, they struggle during the next one. One of the primary functions of Activate, Engage, and Assess is to assess student levels of background knowledge and/or skills necessary for the lesson or unit.

Background knowledge can come in the form of naive preconceptions in science—which a lesson or unit will redirect. Humans are intuitive beings, yet the conclusions they make about the natural world may run contrary to fact. Elaborating and broadening these preconceived notions about the world is a core concept of science instruction. Students naturally want to explain or make sense of their observations. Educators want to help them enlarge and appropriately generalize their conceptual knowledge. Take, for example, the study of the life cycle of plants. An incorrect notion some students may bring to plant life-cycle study is that leaves change color due to a drop in temperature, which runs contrary to scientific fact.

Adept science teachers create opening activities where these naive preconceptions are revealed. As the unit progresses, activities are designed to redirect student conceptual understanding.

Tapping into background knowledge itself needs not always be a complex task. Sometimes all that is needed is that background knowledge is engaged so students' interest is hooked and they have some basis to relate to the lesson. Teachers are simply looking for ways to make the upcoming lesson relevant to the students, and they don't want to leave that connection to chance.

When teaching *The House on Mango Street*, for example, an English teacher may hook student interest by asking them to tap into their own personal experience before they start reading.[2] The teacher is looking to hook students' interest and engage them in the lesson through some relevant tie to their lives. Students could be asked to answer the prompts found immediately below, then share their experiences in a large- or small-group discussion setting. The prompts might sound like these:

- In what areas of your life do you have the most freedom to do what you want?
- In what parts do you have the least freedom?
- To what degree does gender, race, religion, education, age, and upbringing play in limiting an individual's personal freedom?

These are important themes in one section of *Mango Street*, and it is important to get students thinking about them up front. Most students should be able to tap into their own experiences to share their ideas. This opening activity assures that students have some background tie to their reading.

By starting with provocative questions that underlie the chapter's themes, teachers engage student interest and activate their background knowledge—which is something most students can access from their own personal experience. Further, by later having students compare and contrast their life experiences with *Mango Street*'s main character, they create interest in the content and increase retention of material.

This is a simple Activate, Engage, and Assess activity built around a topic that taps the background knowledge every student has. By tapping into personal background knowledge, teachers create relevance for the topic to be studied and uncover personal experiences that students can bring to their learning activities.

While an Activate, Engage, and Assess activity should include an enticing activity to hook student interest, it usually needs to include some form of formative assessment where teachers measure the students' levels of background knowledge or entry skills necessary for success in the lesson.

If students do not fare well on this diagnostic assessment, teachers need to help students create background knowledge or build skills before they begin the lesson. Oftentimes, students simply forget critical content from previous study, which must be reviewed. In other instances, skills or content knowledge may need to be augmented before some students are able to take meaningful steps forward in their learning.

For multiday lessons or units, Activate, Engage, and Assess may simply be an activity that relates to the work that was completed in the last lesson. This could mean opening with a problem like the one studied in the previous lesson or a quick answer-and-recall activity where students review material from the day before. Teachers can start with prompts that all students must answer and then, through a small- or large-group activity, share answers with a larger group.

Teachers can assess to what degree material was learned from the previous day by doing a quick check of the students' written answers (electronic responders work wonderfully here). This is also the point where teachers decide whether to reteach part of the previous lesson or move ahead and assist students who did not quite "get it." In either scenario, teachers understand that students will not progress unless they are ready to take the next step.

What happens when students don't have the background knowledge or skills necessary to successfully complete a lesson? If a large part of the class is missing skills and knowledge, then perhaps whole-group activities are needed to provide them before the lesson or unit moves ahead. If only a small number falls short, then teachers can differentiate instruction through grouping students around similar skill levels or conceptual understanding, which will be discussed later in the chapter.

The key, though, is that teachers do not move forward with the lesson until they have solid evidence that the majority of students are prepared for success. They also need to implement a strategy to help students who need assistance. If students are not ready for the lesson or unit ahead, they will struggle with the material and, most likely, fall short of their potential for success.

In the Madeline Hunter era, teachers designed lesson openers to hook student interest. With an Activate, Engage, and Assess activity, teachers not only engage interest, they tap background knowledge and assess to what degree students are ready to move ahead with the lesson or unit.

Importance of Background Knowledge

Students bring varied levels of background knowledge (sometimes none) to a classroom activity, and a lack of understanding can seriously impede their ability to learn. In his book *Building Background Knowledge for Academic Achievement*, Robert Marzano states, "Students who have a great deal of background knowledge in a given subject area are likely to learn new information readily and quite well. The converse is also true."[3]

Take, for example, a family who coupled their Disney World vacation with a visit to the Kennedy Space Center, about an hour's drive away. During their visit, the family's middle-school-age daughter walked through the center's exhibits, toured the Rocket Garden (which is filled with pioneer rockets and spacecraft), walked through the space shuttle mock-up, took the bus trip to the launch-pad viewing gantry, and visited the Saturn V Building, which displays a complete moon rocket. Wouldn't that student be likely to succeed in a unit on space exploration at school a month later?

While this may be an extreme example, ample background knowledge on a topic can significantly enhance a learning experience. Unfortunately, not all homes are filled with families who travel extensively. Many homes may be devoid of the newspapers, magazines, technology, discussions, and even the vocabulary that arm students with relevant background concepts for their studies. Many homes lack meaningful dinnertime conversations.

Students who suffer from lack of background knowledge are often children who come from poverty, since their experiences are often limited. Marzano continues, "The most straight forward way to enhance students' academic background knowledge is to provide academically enriching experiences, particularly for students whose home environments do not do so naturally."[4]

An illustration of broad background knowledge is the ability to process the allusions found in reading. If, for example, a newspaper article is referring to a political candidate as "possibly the Harry Truman of the race," a reader with adequate historical background knowledge would conclude that the candidate may pull out a stunning victory at the end.

Allusions like this run rich in quality writing. Without some knowledge of American history in the late 1940s, though, the Harry Truman example is meaningless for students.

What is important to remember is that our students most likely have a vast quantity of background knowledge stored in their memories—it just may not be the kind teachers can tap for understanding for academic purposes. While students may be lacking in the proper prior knowledge for an activity, given their life experience and background, that lack of background knowledge should never be mistaken for lack of intelligence. Oftentimes, though, students' knowledge provides a foundation to build upon.

Take, for example, the concept of numbers. During a math lesson, for example, an elementary teacher asks her students to count backward from 100. One youngster raises her hand and answers that the next number would be 59. While this may not have been the correct answer for this activity, the teacher doesn't chastise the student but rather chooses to explore her reasoning. When the teacher probes further, the student explains that on her home microwave timer, 59 comes after 100. The skillful teacher acknowledges that when dealing with time, :59 does come after 1:00 when a digital timer counts backwards. Rather than allowing the student to be confused about her world, the math teacher honors her prior knowledge (which in the context of time was correct) but redirects the learning back toward numbers and away from measuring time.

Do students need to experience things firsthand to create powerful background knowledge? Certainly not. Textbooks, newspaper and magazine articles, electronic encyclopedias, websites, and Wikipedia can all be great sources for "filling in" missing background knowledge.

Depending upon the topic, even students with a reasonable breadth of experience may need to have prior knowledge supplemented before they can fully begin to understand the content that lies ahead. Take the ubiquitously taught novel *To Kill a Mockingbird,* for example.[5] To understand fully the dire circumstances of Tom Robinson and appreciate the noble actions of the protagonist Atticus Finch, students *really* need to understand the racism that existed in America (in both the North and the South) nearly three-quarters of a century ago. Knowledge of

Jim Crow and other forms of discrimination are essential to a thorough understanding of *To Kill a Mockingbird.*

If the students don't have it, the teacher needs to provide it. *Mockingbird*'s enduring understandings are only fully understood through thorough background knowledge of that era.

Electronic sources—television, video tape, and video streaming—can be exceptional ways for the stay-in-town student to experience the world. While Marzano believes that "one of the most straightforward ways to generate virtual experiences" is through reading—something most teachers would agree with—experiencing visual mediums like educational television and video can be a powerful tool to enhance the development of background knowledge as well.[6]

The Activate, Engage, and Assess portion of a lesson should be designed to hook student interest and activate and assess background knowledge. Teachers need to be prepared to assess background knowledge and supplement it and other skills to a sufficient level so that the student may function well when performing the lesson. This will require that teachers differentiate instruction. Without supplementing inadequate knowledge or skill base, though, students are set up for unnecessary challenge in an upcoming activity.

In literacy, understanding vocabulary is a form of background knowledge key to student success. Assignments may contain vocabulary new to students. Without an adequate understanding of this vocabulary, the students may struggle and stumble. Front loading vocabulary study before reading or study begins gives students the tools they need to be successful in the lesson.

In science, experiencing phenomena before naming it is a form of background knowledge. For example, students would observe single-celled organisms in pond water under a microscope. They would observe their behavior and write down questions that come to mind. "Why do they swim around?" students may wonder, or "Where do they get their energy?" Once the students have experienced a single cell at work, the science teacher delves into studying what actually makes up a cell and how it functions. The teacher has created the background knowledge necessary to make sense of this lesson.

Whether introducing a unit that is weeks in length or a lesson that my take a class an hour to complete, it is essential that teachers activate student interest and engage and assess background knowledge and skills. To have students enter a lesson without the necessary knowledge or skills is to risk dooming them to struggle.

No carpenter, surgeon, or electrician would consider attempting a job without the appropriate tools. The purpose of Activate, Engage, and Assess is to make sure students have the appropriate tools to perform the task. If those tools do not yet exist, teachers must find ways to provide them so that students can be successful.

Simply, students need more of a warm up than "Open your books to chapter 6" if they are to master the required content. At the beginning of each lesson, unit, or experiment, teachers need to hook interest, engage background knowledge, and assess required skills and prior understanding. In short, through an Activate, Engage, and Assess activity, teachers need to *intentionally* make sure students are prepared for the content that lies ahead.

The Reflective Teacher

- When I begin a unit or lesson, how do I hook student interest and assess the level of skills and background knowledge my students bring with them?
- To what degree do I make sure that my students are armed with background knowledge and key skills necessary for success before they begin a lesson or unit?

EXPLORE, DISCOVER, AND DIFFERENTIATE

No educator would argue with the fact that students need to learn a tremendous amount of content knowledge. A critical question to ask, though, is "How do teachers make content stick?" The traditional ways to impart content knowledge is through lecture or textbook reading. While this is an expedient way to impart information, is it the best method to transit long-term knowledge in a manner that students can understand and manipulate for future use in their own lives?

Consider what Pascal, the great French philosopher, mathematician, and physicist said: "People are generally better persuaded by the reasons which they have discovered than by those which have come into the minds of others." Think about life's most valuable learning experiences. Are they those lessons that others passed on in the form of advice? Or are they lessons where individuals learned experiences, information, and wisdom on their own?

For many students (present and past), the material that was presented to them—through reading or lectures—was learned for immediate use, typically for the test, then largely forgotten. Learning experiences that required active participation, though, are ones students have a greater chance of remembering, just as one would have a greater chance of remembering a city if they visited it and walked the streets, as opposed to just reading about it in a book.

This author's experience working with teachers to develop inquiry-based, hands-on activities has shown this instructional method's value. During one series of trainings on measurement with elementary math teachers, for example, the instruction was delivered through hands-on, inquiry-based lessons. Prior to the training, teachers relied upon textbooks and worksheets to compare and contrast the English and the metric systems of measurement. As a result of the training, teachers created activities where students measured, weighed, and filled common items.

Students spent math sessions moving around the classroom measuring desks, book cases, and textbooks. They filled bottles, jars, and jugs with water, charting the capacity. They weighed pencils and books. In the process, students created charts to compare and contrast these different systems, and the student results were analyzed through rich discussions.

Through these hands-on activities, the students *discovered* that there are about three centimeters to an inch, and a yard and a meter are pretty close in length. They also discovered that a liter of water weighs a kilogram, which led to a discussion about why this might occur: the metric system is intentional by design. These were a messy couple of days of learning. Students were very active measuring items and water was spilled—but the results were very tidy. When students were tested on measurement on the state-mandated test months later, the school results showed remarkably improved understanding. Of the schools that used this inquiry method of instruction, *all* schools showed increases in their measurement test scores over the previous years' results.

The heart of Construct Meaning is to replicate similar inquiry process during the Explore, Discover, and Differentiate phase of lessons. Its purpose is to use activities that make kids think, to explore and discover their understanding. This gathering of information, through methods like experimentation, research, or collaborative analysis (or a mixture of all these), is at the heart of the exploration process.

Equally important, though, is the problem-solving process itself. Students learn to construct their own understanding of the world through guidance from their teacher. By using problem-solving techniques, they learn to become independent, lifelong learners. In short, they *learn* how to learn.

This is where the teaching philosophy described in this book breaks with more traditional methods. For many, their high school and college learning environment required that they read and absorb information that was presented to them in the form of readings, lectures, and movies. Chances are this method worked for many educators, and because their educational experiences were positive and successful, they returned to the classroom to teach in a similar fashion.

Lecture or explanation is something most teachers feel comfortable doing. Unfortunately, school is not a successful experience for many young people. About a quarter of incoming freshmen at high schools across the country do not graduate with a diploma. Might a contributing factor be the way educational institutions teach? Is having kids read, listen, absorb, then recall for a test the best method of instruction? Does this method build a sense of content relevance in students? Does it *really* prepare them to think and function in the future?

What if education were different? What if the purpose of core educational strategies was to deliver content through methods that directed students to problem solve and ponder—in other words, to make kids think, as was discussed in Principle 1.

This is not to say that lecture, reading, worksheets, and other traditional ways of imparting knowledge are not useful. Learning that requires students to explore and discover can be time intensive. Sometimes the most expedient way to deliver simple content is simply to deliver it.

When studying grammar, for example, a teacher could design activities where students discover what a noun or a verb is, but given all that they need to cover in a school year, this may not be a worthy use of class time. For parts of speech, giving students the definitions would be the expedient thing to do.

On the other hand, when teachers want to improve students' writing style, lecturing them on the use of "strong verbs and specific nouns" might be a less effective way of covering this concept than creating an activity where students analyze samples of strong writing and weak writing and discover for themselves that the reason for stylistic superiority is the presence of powerful verbs and descriptive nouns.

In the end, a primary goal of our system is to build content knowledge and the capacity to problem solve and think as an individual. Content knowledge that lasts can be solidly constructed through the Explore and Discover format.

Discussed below are some examples of Explore and Discover activities that make kids think.

Discover Understanding: Go Greek

Socrates was renowned for asking questions. Rather than lecture students, the ancient Greek master would ask carefully crafted questions that would lead students to an understanding of their own. While this method is very teacher centered, the student, with the instructor's guidance, does the exploring and discovering.

The Socratic form of discussion is one of teaching's oldest techniques for constructing meaning. The purpose of Socratic questioning is to get students to turn here and go there in their thinking, to intellectually walk the corridors of concepts until they arrive at an understanding. Questions are thoughtfully posed. If students don't respond in the expected manner, the question is reframed. Depending upon the desired outcome, questions continue to be crafted until the teacher directs the students to a desired understanding. When using this Socratic technique, the teacher is limited to only asking questions. The students do the thinking and pondering.

Age old and time tested, Socratic inquiry is an extremely effective method of exploring and discovering, but it often relies upon some form of content for students to probe for new understanding. In a philosophy class, that may be personal experience or previous learning.

In a history class, it may mean constructing a series of questions that will uncover the significance of a specific event. The limitation of the Socratic method is that content of some form has to exist first before this questioning strategy can be utilized.

The Socratic method can be used in class discussions, but it can also be utilized daily when assisting students with questions they may have regarding their class activities. Adept math teachers, for example, give an answer directly only as the last resort. When students ask questions while doing their math, these teachers respond with questions. This math teacher identifies what the student knows, then frames questions to take them step-by-step to new understanding. These teachers know where students get lost. They frame the questions necessary to get students unstuck.

The same strategy applies to reading. When students get stumped uncovering the meaning of a challenging passage of text, rather than give students the interpretation, adept teachers of reading ask questions that carefully lead students to discover the meaning on their own.

While full-fledged Explore and Discover can be time intensive, Socratic questioning in all its forms isn't, especially on a one-to-one basis. Simply, when a student asks a question during an activity, answer it with a question. Don't deliver the information. Ask probing questions to get the students to come to their own understanding. Tap into previous learning or real-life experiences. Question, so that students explore and discover the answer.

As a group activity, Socratic seminars are a fishbowl strategy where students do the discussing among themselves based on questions the teacher has posed and the ideas and controversy students generate themselves. In a Socratic seminar, four to five students are seated in the middle of the class, with the remaining students circled around them. An additional seat—an open one—is placed in the middle as well. The students in the "hot seats" in the middle discuss the Socratic questions the teacher has created. The teacher observes and only redirects discussion if students get sidetracked.

In a Socratic seminar, only those in the middle may speak; those students circled around take notes on the discussion. If a student wants to make a comment or join the discussion, he or she must take the open seat in the middle. At that time, a single student may leave a "hot seat" and return to the outer circle. All students seated in the middle must participate before they can leave for the outer circle. A participation score can be given to students to encourage and assess participation.

Nun Thing discussions were developed by the Teacher Leadership Project and used near the conclusion of their multiday technology workshops as a tool for reflection. Called the Nun Thing because the activity originated in a convent, this discussion format can be a tremendously powerful means of debriefing provocative reading or study. The Nun Thing functions like a Socratic seminar, but the center-circle participants are limited to three in the hot seats with one left open. Again, only those in the center may participate.

With the Nun Thing, though, no Socratic-style questions are used to prime discussion. Students are free to choose the topic or issue they desire. It just needs to relate to the study at hand. While the teacher may step in to stir discussion when needed, the Nun Thing is in a sense more student directed since students are the ones driving discussion from the beginning.

An effective way to introduce the Socratic seminars or the Nun Thing to students new to this format is to show videos of excellent past discussions. Whether teachers use Socratic questioning or facilitate Socratic or Nun Thing discussion seminars, students are the ones who are doing the exploring to discover and create their own understanding.

Scaffolding the Thinking Process

Sometimes, students don't have the strategies to explore and discover on their own. As a result, teachers need to carefully scaffold the thinking process so that students learn to be independent thinkers and learners.

If Explore and Discover comes in the form of research, teachers can provide graphic organizers, templates, and vetted websites to guide students to the required understanding. In general, the younger the student, the more structure necessary to carry on productive, frustration-free research. Typically, students lack the capabilities for full-blown Explore and Discover research until their high school years.

Scaffolds can also guide the Explore and Discover process by teaching analysis strategies. Poetry and short stories can be analyzed by students in small groups using scaffolded analysis strategies. Two strategies, TP-CASTT (pronounced Tip Cast) and SOAPSTones, used by the College Board, give students a series of steps in which they can dissect literature, analyze its components, then synthesize an interpretation, the goal being to understand its meaning and significance.

SOAPSTones—an acronym standing for Speaker, Occasion, Audience, Purpose, Subject, Tone—can be used to scaffold analysis skill for literary text. TP-CASTT analysis—Title, Paraphrase, Connotation, Attitude, Shifts, Title, and Theme—lead students from a surface analysis of the poem to its deeper meaning (theme) through carefully scripted prompts.[7]

Scaffolds, as discussed in Principle 3: Nurture Student Learning, are strategies and organizers teachers provide students to help them shape their learning. Students use the scaffolds, internalize them, then personalize them for their own use. Cognitive strategies like TP-CASTT and SOAPSTones give students a regimented way to analyze and understand complex literature to start.

With practice, though, these steps become so ingrained and personalized in students' minds that they can explore challenging selections and discover their meaning without giving thought to the steps it took to get there. These scripted activities direct students to explore and discover their own understanding of literature.

Developing scientific conceptual understanding can be handled the same way through exploratory projects and experiments. Methods of explorations emulate the scientific process so that students, as they conduct experiments, practice scientific inquiry in a methodical, structured format. Likewise, lab reports can be formatted to ensure that students conduct their thinking, analysis, and synthesis like trained scientists would. Again, as students participate in guided or open inquiry, they are conducting explorations to discover scientific concepts and to examine and refine their own preconceptions—they are just supported in a way that prompts them to develop conceptual understanding in a logical fashion. Effective science teachers create activities that help students become independent learners by scaffolding sound scientific thinking.

Freedom to Differentiate Instruction:
A Benefit of Explore and Discover

While having students explore and discover their own understandings is in and of itself a valuable learning process, the act of having class activities focused on tasks produces one productive outcome: It gives teachers freedom to work with students who need help.

In traditional classrooms, teachers spend large amounts of time in front of their classes delivering content, explaining skills, or leading large-group discussion. When teachers place themselves at the center of classroom activities, they limit the time they have on hand to assist students who need help. This method leaves little time for working with students one-on-one or in small groups. If teachers want to really help all students learn, they have to carve time out of instruction to offer assistance.

When educators create activities where students are working to discover and create their own understanding, teachers become free to offer students help individually or in groups. This is an ideal time to apply the skills of Stiggins' "assessment *for* learning" discussed in Principle 3: Nurture Student Learning. Teachers can look at the work being produced. Where the work is not up to standard, teachers can assist students to improve their understanding.

Certainly, comments on paper, quizzes, and lab reports written by teachers during prep times or their off-hours are valuable, but this face-to-face, "just in time" interaction can be invaluable in redirecting thinking. Differentiated instruction for other types of skill or content deficits can be conducted as well.

Explore and Discover activities also free teachers to provide meaningful feedback and assistance for students when returning tests, papers, or reports. They can discuss students' work and progress. Students can reflect on their progress and, with their teacher, plan what next steps need to be taken.

Exploring and discovering is essentially that: Students are actively engaged in creating their own learning. Whatever the method used, students are independent workers (either individually or in groups) during Explore and Discover. The teacher serves as facilitator of understanding.

The Reflective Teacher

- In my classroom, how do my lessons direct students to gather and analyze information?
- How am I building research-and-analysis skills that will serve students in their adult lives?

SYNTHESIZE AND INTEGRATE

The opening of this chapter discussed how writing has a beginning, middle, and end—each with its specific purpose. Effective stories are those with endings that tie up loose ends and leave readers satisfied. The same is true for music and movies. The truth is this: Endings matter.

This is especially true in classrooms. Rushed to get everything done, teachers may feel forced to speed up a unit to complete it on time—skipping what might be very valuable activities to assure the content was covered (which begs the question, was content *really retained*?). Nearly every educator has experienced this pressure at some time. In the end, by shortening the closing of their lessons and units, teachers may be leaving the learning undone.

Think about what teachers want students to take away from a lesson and how long they want students to retain the learning. Their assumption may be that as students move through the lesson, they gather content and place it in some neat cubicle in their mind for future reference, but that may not be the case for most students unless there is some striking need for the content or skills presented to them.

Most students work to retain learning for the purpose of the test or final product. Unfortunately, students often lose much of the content afterward. The outcome of education should be more than this.

What if the summative assessment for a lesson or a unit did more than require students to memorize or practice for the purpose of recall of content and skills? What if teachers asked for a *relevant* application of learning?

Authentic learning requires a relevant performance assessment that brings understanding of content to the surface for teachers to assess (summative assessment, a.k.a., Stiggins' "assessment *of* learning"). The stage of the lesson—Synthesize and Integrate—is meant to do just that: organize student thinking and integrate it into a form that is useful and retainable.

This final task is meant, whenever possible, to incorporate as many learning styles as possible (visual, auditory, kinesthetic), hit the higher level of Bloom's Taxonomy (analysis, synthesis, and/or evaluation), and incorporate a variety of skills.

The close of the lesson is meant to *synthesize* all the students have learned in the lesson or unit and *integrate* this content or these skills into products that are useful, relevant, long lasting, and enjoyable.

Performance Tasks

If the aim in education is to prepare students for the real world, then perhaps teachers need to be more creative than just ending a unit with a test. Sure, this statement may give some teachers heartburn, but looking at adult life, what is more prized, rote knowledge or actual performance?

A real-life application of this concept is getting a driver's license. When teens desire their driver's license, they are required to complete a basic test of rules and skills of the road before they take their test of driving skills. Driving rules can be easily memorized in an evening, but the skills of driving safely are much more complex and reflect a deeper understanding of knowledge.

For teens to become safe drivers, they need to log many hours behind the wheel of the car with an adept driver alongside to guide them until they become proficient at their skills. While students may pass their driving-rules written test, they may still be incompetent drivers—despite near-perfect scores on the written test. Years of good driving (a performance task), however, imply that rules of the road are known, but more importantly, that they be applied correctly in the actual setting. A simple written test would not provide ample evidence of driving skills. It is performance that matters.

Likewise, aspiring professionals take tests for their securities' or realtor's license, for example, but obtaining certification doesn't guarantee success in the field. A test typically measures only content knowledge. Again, they may ace the test but end up selling few homes or making poor stock picks for customers. Regardless of their knowledge base, they may end up losing their job for poor actual performance. Whether selling homes or mutual funds, it is the application of knowledge through actual performance that determines success. Shouldn't classrooms function like this as much as possible too?

While "traditional" assessment methods certainly have their place in teaching, performance tasks, as identified, are a much more complex and rich way to assess understanding. Effective performance tasks give students options. They are either very open-ended in their design, or a variety of options are provided to students. Performance tasks are meant to be inclusive. Students, no matter their skill level, should be able to complete the performance task, although a lack of content understanding will most likely appear in the final product. Rubrics are given to students at the beginning of the task so they know the learning targets that must be met.

Two styles of performance task are designed to place students in real-world settings. One style of task is designed around the acronym of RAFT:[8]

R = Role and context
A = Audience to address
F = Format
T = Topic about which to write

The RAFT is designed to give students a creative form of expression, although the teacher is the one who typically sets the parameters. One RAFT can be set for the class (say, for a social-studies summative assessment), but a variety of topics can be assigned if needed.

For example, if social-studies students were to synthesize and integrate their understanding of World War II (WWII), a RAFT for the unit might look like this:

Role: Students become American GI soldiers in the European theater.
Audience: Parents and friends at home.
Form: Personal letters sent home describing the overall events.
Topic: Key battles and tough living conditions on the battlefront from 1944 to 1945.

Since WWII included more facets that just the European battle, additional RAFTs could be created around Rosie the Riveter, Japanese-American internment, battles of the Pacific theater, dropping the atomic bombs on Japan, racial discrimination, the Tuskegee airmen, and the role of women in the military. By creating an array of RAFTs, a broad variety of aspects of a unit can be covered.

Wiggins and McTighe's *Understanding by Design* creates performance tasks by following a slightly different guide: GRASPS.[9] The term GRASPS is an acronym, meaning the following:

G = Goal
R = Role
A = Audience
S = Situation
P = Products
S = Standards for Success

A GRASPS breaks the tasks into more defined parts and requires the addition of standards for success (rubrics and checklists), but it essentially functions the same way. Typically, all class members are directed by the same GRASPS. Students express their individuality through the variety of products they create. If teachers want to increase the cognitive challenge of the GRASPS, they can create stakeholder groups for the Role and require students to create final projects that align with that specific group's values and beliefs.

Rather than creating an artificial lab setting, for example, an earth-science teacher opts instead to collect samples of water from above and below sources of possible pollution on the river that flows through their city—as was discussed in Principle 2: Teach Big Ideas. The big idea in the lesson is to teach students the value of river stewardship. A GRASPS for a science unit on water quality might look like this:

Goal: To identify point and nonpoint sources of pollution on a two-mile stretch of your local river.

Role: You are a science consultant hired by an environmental group called the Friends of the River.

Audience: Representatives from the state Department of Ecology, who will be in town holding a hearing on the river's health.

Situation: Fish and insect life has been declining in the local river over the last two decades and algae blooms have appeared. Your team has been hired by Friends of the River to identify possible sources of pollution.

Products: A report that measures increases in pollution and decreases in dissolved oxygen as the river flows past different sources of pollution.

Standards for Success: Measurement of Water Quality rubric.

Whether organized around a RAFT or a GRASP, a performance task places students in situations where they have to function as they might in a real-life setting. Providing models/examples of quality work, though, is crucial for students to meet learning outcomes.

By their nature, performance tasks are great ways to differentiate instruction. No matter their skill or ability level, students should be able to participate at some level. Performance tasks can also have a surprising outcome. Low performers on traditional tests, allowed to work on their own and express their creativity, can become high achievers on performance tasks. Constructed properly, performance tasks give students the chance to express their individuality through their final creation.

There is no question that carefully crafted test or essay prompts can make students think and are accurate ways to gauge student understanding. Given the demands pressing upon teachers these days, these tests and essays are a time-efficient way to assess understanding.

Where these methods fall short is in their artificial, academic nature. Unless adults are attempting some form of professional certification, few professionals have their understanding tested in a paper-and-pencil method after they leave school. In real life, most knowledge is tested through performance—something that represents a rich mix of understanding. If educators want their schools to be preparation for "real life," then they need to embed "real life" performance measures into their classrooms.

Application of Thinking

Learning, to be relevant to students, must allow for application. Learning in isolation will remain fragmented and will most likely be forgotten. Learning that is applied stands a better chance of being retained.

Not every unit lends itself to a performance task. Sometimes time frames and content require less complex assessment. Still, learning can be synthesized and integrated through application as long as these final assessment activities "make kids think."

Take, for example, the learning of literary devices such as theme, conflict, and characterization studied in language-arts class. For the unit assessment, teachers could create a matching-answer test to link literary terms to their definitions and develop a bank of multiple-choice questions to check for student understanding of the terms as they apply to the short stories just read in the unit. This would require recall of the content—a low-level thinking skill.

If, however, teachers were to give their class a fresh story and ask the students to apply their understanding of literary terms, the learners would have to comprehend the definition of the terms and analyze the text to identify examples of use. With this method, literary devices become tools students use to better understand text.

Similarly, American-history teachers can end a unit on WWII with a comprehension test that includes recall questions about Japanese-American discrimination and internment. But would this test really evaluate student knowledge about how nations react during times of fear?

A more complex, yet more realistic, way to assess whether students can synthesize and integrate their understanding might be to ask them to research and critique treatment of Muslim Americans in the years following the September 11 attacks. Students could compare and contrast treatment of these two ethnic groups and evaluate to what degree America learned the lessons of WWII.

Students can apply the lessons they learn in applied physics to their own physical safety. Through exploratory activities, students learn that velocity and energy have an exponential relationship: When you double your velocity, you quadruple the energy, for example. Students applying this concept to driving identify that while a car moving at 20 mph may take x distance to stop, a vehicle moving at 60 mph will take nine times x distance to bring to a halt.

Learning, to be retained, must be relevant and reusable. Assessing students' ability to apply their learning to new situations gives teachers insight into the degree students synthesize and integrate their learning.

Revision of Thinking

Sometimes, a shift in the way students view the world or subject matter is the outcome teachers desire. In subjects like history, math, and science, an effective way to check for student integration of learning is by having them return to their original hypothesis or understanding and to either support their original ideas or revise them based on the learning that has taken place in the lesson or unit.

Teachers can use the Activate, Engage, and Assess portion of the lesson to measure student preconceptions of the topic to be studied. In a social-studies unit on the Civil War, for example, the history teacher might open by asking students to write a paragraph about the causes of this great conflict. Most students will answer that the war was fought to abolish slavery.

While this was the outcome of the war, the fear of abolition of slavery prompted the war, and the desire to keep the Union united motivated Lincoln in the beginning far more than his repugnance of the institution of slavery. The southern states' desire to direct their destiny, and the damage abolition would cause their economies, were also determining factors in the war. This shift from a simplified view of history to a more complex understanding of the currents that stir it is an important outcome in understanding of the past. Appropriate assessment will judge the degree to which the shift has taken place.

Likewise, in a physics lesson on falling objects, the science teacher might ask students in the Activate, Engage, and Assess activity to hypothesize what might happen when a cannonball is allowed to free-fall from an elevation of 10,000 feet. A common, naive preconception students may have is that the sphere would continue to accelerate. A carefully crafted experiment as an Explore and Discover activity (like the one which will be described later in this chapter) would reveal that the cannonball would accelerate until at some point, due to air resistance, it would reach terminal velocity, and constant speed would be maintained.

In science, appearances can be deceiving. This shift away from how the world appears to how it actually functions is a foundation of good science instruction.

Assessing the degree to which shifts in thinking take place can be an important component to the Synthesize and Integrate part of a lesson.

The Reflective Teacher

- How do I assess understanding in relevant ways that engage students and require higher cognition and a complex mix of skills?
- How do I make student learning stick beyond the next test?
- How do I ensure that students' misunderstanding and naive preconceptions have been revised by the end of a lesson or unit?

The Power of Technology

Throughout human history, technology has changed the way humans live and view their world. Probably no greater example of this exists than the changes that have been brought (or wrought, depending upon your perspective) by electronic technology in the last two decades. The Internet, personal networking sites, iPods, cell phones, etc., have revolutionized the way people view the world and interact with one another.

Technology, though, has also created a divide: Students growing up with this technology embedded in their lives (digital natives) live in a vastly different world from their older teachers and parents, who either reject it, don't understand it, or only dabble in it. Technology has changed the way our young people live and think; its highly stimulating nature most likely has reduced their ability to endure mundane tasks. But the change is a reality educators must live with and adapt to if the educational system is to be effective.

In many ways, the traditional classroom of read the book, listen to the lecture, answer the worksheets, and finish the test is extremely outmoded given how today's student-mind functions. It is like asking students to take a wagon train to their learning when jet airliners are available.

The concept of "Construct Meaning" can be a technologically rich and relevant way for students to learn. Video, video streaming, interactive games, and informational Internet sites can be powerful ways to build the background knowledge and skills students may need to be successful in lessons or units. Placing these sources on a website makes them available any time students or teachers need to access them.

When completing research, Internet sources and resource sites like ProQuest provide instant access to information. Today, research that two decades ago would take weeks to complete can be finished in an evening. In science and math classes, probes give students immediate measurement simply not available through the human senses. In mathematics, a calculator (also called a handheld computer) provides a graph instantly for a function that formerly would have taken hours to complete. Learning and understanding are accelerated.

Digital photo- and video-editing software opens up vast creative opportunities for students when these applications are applied to projects. The interesting thing about use of applications like these is that students who sometimes flounder when completing traditional classroom tasks produce high-quality work when technology is involved. Rather than being seen as drudge work, technology-driven performance tasks deeply engage students. After all, students are functioning in *their* world when they perform these tasks.

Technology can also add another layer of complexity to projects. With multimedia software, students can pan a photo or focus on a particular aspect of it—a deeper form of interpretation and communication than presenting a regular photo on poster board. The intonation of the voice in the voice-overs adds another layer of interpretation. Positive events call for an upbeat voice; somber ones call for a sober tone. When adding music, the appropriate choice enhances the project. Serious proceedings require solemn music; adventurous actions call for a buoyant melody; enjoyable events justify something whimsical. Photos, text, graphics, voice-overs, and music all work together to deliver the content to the audience. Multimedia software takes projects to new levels. The great thing about most entry-level software is it is easy to use. In the end, a good multimedia project reflects a comprehensive understanding of a topic.

Something as simple as a document camera and an interactive whiteboard (such as Smart or Promethean boards) have the power to create classrooms where students "construct meaning." When examining student work, for example, teachers can place the document or problem under a document camera or on an interactive whiteboard and actually analyze as a class what is working and what is not. The positive difference in student engagement is powerful.

Constructing meaning using technology creates powerful learning environments. For technology to effectively impact classroom instruction, though, it needs to be at the heart of classroom activities and instruction, not just an occasional add-on.

REFLECT AND REVISE

While technically not a part of the lesson, reflecting and revising is a key component to creating the most effective educational experience possible for students. No lesson, no matter how well crafted, is entirely perfect. All need revision, and the process is ongoing.

Even as lessons or units unfold, adept teachers work revising prompts or tweaking procedures to get the results they desire from students. Teachers reflect on the questions being asked by students or the struggles they are facing, and they revise the lesson, sometimes in the middle of class, to assure the most productive learning experience possible. In some ways teachers are like chefs: They sample and spice until they get the flavor they desire.

If a lesson is well crafted, the content engaging, and the challenge appropriate, most students will learn and make progress. A great problem arises, though, when teachers opt to blame the students for lack of progress. Improper parenting, problem peers, and poor motivation can all be used as excuses to explain why students are not on track in a classroom. While these may all be factors, lessons and teaching practice should be of a caliber to overcome these challenges for most students.

For teachers to improve student performance, they must be honest in the assessment of what led to success and what caused the lesson or unit to fall short. Reflection, though, needs to be forthright. What went well? What didn't? Did the majority of students achieve the desired outcome? What can be done for those who didn't? How could the lesson be revised to improve it?

Classroom practice, too, needs to be a constant assessment of where the students are in their skills and content, what activities are necessary to boost them, and how lessons and classroom practice can be improved in order to achieve this. Teachers need to constantly reflect on their lessons and practice and revise them to improve the learning environment.

THE PROCESS OF CONSTRUCTING MEANING: THREE MODEL LESSONS

So far in this chapter, the stages of Construct Meaning have been dealt with using isolated examples. Found below are examples of how the concepts of Activate, Engage, and Assess; Explore and Discover; and Synthesize and Integrate appear in three different learning activities.

Constructing Meaning: An Elementary-Level Writing Workshop

In order to create more description in students' writing, an elementary teacher wants to introduce the idea of adjectives. Many of her students are writing simple sentences with nouns and verbs and few adjectives. The teacher opens her lesson by addressing her students in the role she wishes them to play.

"Writers, today we're going to work on ways to add more details to your writing so that it makes clear mental images for your readers. We want them to be able to close their eyes and see your wonderful details through your words."

The teacher then hands out a simple paragraph which has a few details in the text. By using this paragraph, she wants to activate their background knowledge, engage their thinking, and assess what they may already know.

With the paragraph distributed, she says, "Please circle the places where the writer adds details to the writing that allow you to imagine what he is talking about. Discuss the writing sample in table teams to make sure you identify all the details."

As the students work, the teacher circulates among the students, listening to the conversation, assessing students' understanding of the concept of an adjective, even though they may not use the term yet. After the students finish the activity, the teacher places the writing sample under the document camera, and groups take turn sharing what they have found.

For the Explore and Discover, the teacher gives her students a sample of much more vibrant, descriptive writing. She sets the students to work, circling words and discussing the images they create. At the end of this group activity, the student groups again share out what they have discovered.

She also introduces a concept: "Writers, those descriptive, juicy words that add images to the writing are called adjectives. They add important details to nouns, which we have talked about." The teacher then adds the term "adjective" to the word wall.

The teacher completes the lesson with an activity that synthesizes their learning by integrating it into a relevant final task. "Writers, I would like to have you take the paragraph out that you wrote yesterday about a special place that means a lot to you. With this draft, though, I want you to add more descriptive details—adjectives—that will build images in your readers' minds. I want you to circle what you added and be prepared to tell us why you added it."

The students spend the next 15 to 20 minutes revising their previous drafts. While the students are at work, the teacher circulates around the room, conferencing with students about their writing pieces and sometimes meeting with a small group of students needing the same assistance, differentiating instruction.

The teacher then strategically asks those students using descriptive adjectives well to share their work. After sharing, the teacher summarizes by stressing the importance of descriptive details in writing. "Today and every day, we will be sure to use lots of juicy adjectives in our writing," she concludes.

From start to finish, this activity may have taken about an hour to complete. While the teacher facilitated the process, the students were the ones constructing meaning of the concept of descriptive writing and adjectives through a process of exploring and discovering. The students then synthesized their understanding of adjectives by integrating them into their own writing.

Constructing Meaning: Humanities Tolerance Unit

American colonial history lends itself to contrasts. In the 1690s, Salem, Massachusetts, was wracked by witch hunts that left 19 accused and executed. Less than eight decades later, though, that same region would be a hotbed for a revolution that would protect individual freedom and religion. To contrast these eras and highlight their differences, a humanities teacher is searching for ways that emphasize the intolerance found in their reading of *The Crucible* and the ideals found in the literature of the Enlightenment, the Declaration of Independence, and the Bill of Rights.

When the city's newspaper reports that a local human-rights activist finds a noose on her doorstep, the teacher decides that a unit on tolerance would be the best way to synthesize student understanding of American ideals.

To activate, engage, and assess student interest, the teacher shares with his class a copy of the article that ran in the local newspaper. The article, titled "Human rights activist finds noose on porch," describes how the African American civil-rights leader found a noose on her doorstep and a racial epithet scrawled on the sidewalk before her home. As expected, the students in his culturally diverse humanities class are upset. They express outrage. The humanities teacher knows that this provocative article will serve as a catalyst for great learning.

In the next step of Activate, Engage, and Assess, the teacher then presents to each student a Knowledge Rating Chart. The chart has three columns. In the left-hand column, the teacher has listed eras of racial, ideological, and cultural intolerance: Salem Witch Trials, Jim Crow, the Holocaust, Japanese-American WWII Internment, and McCarthyism and the Red Scare of the 1950s.

In the middle column of the graphic organizer, students, as part of this activity, write what they know or have heard about each era.

Assessing the Knowledge Rating Chart, the teacher sees that the students' Salem boxes show good understanding, but the responses for the other areas are pretty sparse—which he expected. For the project that the teacher has planned, a thorough understanding of times of intolerance is essential. He will use a simple Explore and Discover activity to build a rounded understanding of all the eras.

Before proceeding to the Explore and Discover activity, the humanities instructor shares the essential questions for the unit:

- How do we create a society where differences are tolerated—even celebrated?
- How do we prevent the ostracizing or casting out of those who are different or those whom we may fear?

Next, the teacher shares the *Understanding by Design* GRASPS he created which will guide the unit and the final performance task:

Goal: To educate the public to deter our citizens from mistreating or discriminating against those who are different.

Role: Recent acts of "hate" crimes have the city mayor concerned about her community. She has asked local high school students to create public-service announcements (PSAs) regarding this topic. The PSAs will run on local television stations.

Audience: Teenagers and young adults in the television-viewing area.

Situation: The city has seen an increase in harassment and discrimination against those perceived as being "different." The mayor would like to create more attitudes of tolerance in the community.

Product: Create a one-minute digital infomercial, using a multimedia software. This infomercial will be based on a narrative script and storyboard.

Standards for Success: The final project must:

- Acknowledge the "lesser angels" of our nature: For example, Puritans' intolerance for differences as found in *The Crucible* and other acts of intolerance listed on the Knowledge Rating Chart.
- Educate the viewing public on the "better angels" of our nature: For example, Enlightenment concepts and Declaration of Independence and Bill of Rights ideals.
- Rate a 3 or a 4 on the Crucible for Change Rubric.

The teacher also hands out the checklist that guides the activity, and the class discusses the expectations found on the rubric. By this time, the class period is over.

For the Explore, Discover, and Differentiate section of the unit, the humanities teacher wheels in the mobile computer lab, where, for two class periods, students research Jim Crow, the Holocaust, Japanese-American WWII Internment, and McCarthyism and the Red Scare. The teacher has collected a list of websites. The students must access one of these then find one additional site on their own as resources for these topics. Students also surf the net to find and store images that might be useful for their project.

The objective for the Explore and Discover phase is to fill in the right-hand column on the Knowledge Rating Chart, titled "What I learned." While the students are busy at work, the teacher uses this time to differentiate instruction. He walks among the students, prompting more research and answering questions for students who are having trouble gathering material to fill out the "What I learned" column of their chart. He clarifies any questions the students might have and suggests key wording to help narrow their Internet searches.

After the students have finished their charts (building their background knowledge in the topic), the humanities teacher places students into collaborative groups of three or four and distributes storyboards for students to create their messages. This is where students synthesize their learning about intolerance and the ideals of the Enlightenment and the Declaration of Independence and integrate it into a meaningful, relevant performance task.

These storyboard instructions prompt students to add intros and outros, create text and voice-overs, identify images and appropriate music, and add works cited for the project. Basically, this storyboard scaffolds the elements of the final presentation; it prompts students to add the required elements found on the Crucible for Change Rubric.

The storyboards are also visible evidence of how students are progressing. While they work, the humanities teacher circulates among the groups, assessing the storyboards for the thinking they make visible. By looking at the progress being made, the instructor can differentiate his comments and suggestions, homing in on what each group needs individually.

At this point, the teacher acts as a gatekeeper for content. Multimedia software is engaging and exciting to work with. In other words, it is a nice carrot. Therefore, before students can progress to working with the software, the humanities teacher evaluates the storyboards for content. If the content represented 3s or 4s on the Crucible for Change Rubric, then students are allowed to proceed to producing their digital project. If not, they are asked to complete more research and enrich the content.

When the storyboards are completed, students are allowed to check out computers and, in teams, they begin creating their final multimedia presentation. Each student is assigned certain slides or scenes to create—all must participate in their share of the production. Using the storyboard as a guide, students bring together the visual elements—music, text, and voice-overs—into a final project that they are proud of.

As the final step of the Synthesize and Integrate portion of the unit, each group displays their projects before the class. Other classrooms, staff, parents, and community leaders are invited to attend to reinforce the relevance and importance of this performance task. For grading, the students self-assess their project using the Crucible for Change Rubric, then pass that rubric along to the teacher for final evaluation.

Constructing Meaning: Secondary Physics Falling-Objects Lesson

The behavior of falling objects is one of the most commonly mis-understood concepts in physics—and for good reason. Given that it takes less time for a dropped hammer to hit one's toe rather than, say, a dropped duck wing, one might conclude that steel has a greater gravitational pull than feathers. An experiment in falling objects, however, illustrates the relationship between gravity, mass, and air resistance.

The purpose of Activate, Engage, and Assess for this experiment is to review critical terms and uncover the naive preconceptions students have coming into this activity. The correcting of possible misconceptions about falling objects is a major goal for this activity.

At the beginning of the Activate, Engage and Assess, students are asked to demonstrate their knowledge of the terms "force," "position," "speed," and "acceleration." These concepts have been applied to a previous study, but understanding these terms is a critical foundation for the following activity.

Next, students in teams are asked to create an initial hypothesis about the forces at work on two falling objects—a pumpkin and a sky diver. To create their hypotheses, students are shown a school-made video of a pumpkin being dropped off a school gym and a clip of a skydiver jumping from an airplane then assuming a spread-eagle position. Both clips hook student interest: the skydiver plunging into the abyss; the pumpkin smashing to smithereens on impact.

After viewing the clips numerous times, students go to work iden-tifying the forces at work by creating free-body diagrams—which are simply arrows that show in what direction forces are at work on the objects (gravity would be a down arrow, for example). The students elaborate on their hypothesis using the terms "force," "position," "ve-locity," and "acceleration." This initial sheet is to include a diagram labeled with the terms and a paragraph of explanation elaborating on their hypothesis. They have to create position-versus-time and velocity-versus-time graphs for each falling object.

Finally, students transfer their hypotheses to small whiteboards. Students circle up and, group by group, explain their hypothesis concerning the forces at work and how these two very different objects move. The teacher and fellow students are allowed to ask clarifying questions, but no hypothesis is deemed correct or incorrect.

By completing this activity, the physics teacher reviews key terms and concepts necessary for success in the experiment that is to follow. Further, by asking students to create a hypothesis and explain it, the teacher identifies naive preconceptions that exist in the understanding of individual teams.

In the falling-objects experiment, students discover (rather than being taught through lecture or reading) the forces of physics. The Explore and Discover part of the lesson requires hands-on activities using common objects meant to replicate the forces at work in the activate-and-engage video: a ball and a coffee filter. The ball is meant to replicate the pumpkin, and a paper coffee filter will represent the skydiver for the purposes of the experiment.

To conduct the experiment, a motion sensor is placed at the top of a tall laboratory ring stand facing downward. The motion sensor is plugged into a computer, and computer software measures and charts velocity when the sensor is activated. To gather their data, students drop the ball or coffee filter below this motion sensor then use the data to analyze each situation and develop conceptual understanding. While the students work on their explorations, the teacher is free to move around the classroom, checking data to assess if students are getting helpful information.

Based on their initial hypothesis, students were asked to predict what position-versus-time and velocity-versus-time graphs would look like. Students drop the ball numerous times below the motion sensor until they receive consistent results. After good data are compiled, students are asked to compare and contrast their results against their predictions and answer the following questions:

- How were your predictions and actual results similar? Different?
- What force(s) is/are acting on the falling ball? How do you know?
- What is happening at various points on the graph?

In short, what the students discover is that the ball, when dropped, starts at zero velocity and continues to accelerate.

The experimental process is repeated by dropping a coffee filter below the motion sensor. The same questions are asked. With the coffee-filter drop, though, students discovered different results. By analyzing the graphs, students could see that the coffee filter, like the ball, accelerated, but at some point in the drop, the velocity flatlined on the graphs—the filter had reached "terminal velocity."

In other words, the force of gravity pulling down and the force of air resistance slowing the fall became balanced, and a constant falling velocity was achieved. In the ball drop, the forces were unbalanced—gravity's downward pull was greater than the force of the air resistance slowing the ball (if given enough distance, though, the ball will reach terminal velocity, but that would not happen in this lab setting).

To close Explore, Discover, and Differentiate on the falling-objects experiment, students were asked to predict how the graphs for the falling ball might be different if the sphere were dropped from a much greater height. The Synthesize and Integrate activities for the falling-objects lesson is designed to assess to what degree the experiment has either reinforced previous understanding or resulted in a shift of thinking.

After the students finish their experiments, the teacher asks them to return to their original hypothesis and graphs and evaluate them based on what they have learned through their experimentation. Students are tasked to either rewrite their hypothesis and redraw their graphs while explaining the change in thinking, or tell why their original thinking was correct based on what they just learned. Key to this is incorporating the results from their experiments into their explanation.

After the original hypotheses are addressed, students circle up with their whiteboards and explain to class members how their original thinking was either reinforced or changed by the experiment.

To conclude, students are shown a video of Apollo 15's Dave Scott dropping a feather and a hammer on the moon to reinforce the idea that the effects of gravity's pull are the same on all objects, regardless of weight, so long as air resistance is negligible.

LESSON TITLE:	
TEACHER:	GRADE LEVEL AND CLASS:

BIG IDEAS:
ESSENTIAL QUESTIONS:
STANDARDS:

BLOOM'S LEVELS OF COGNITION: (HIGHLIGHT)

ANALYSIS	KNOWLEDGE
SYNTHESIS	COMPREHENSION
EVALUATION	APPLICATION

TYPE(S) OF RIGOR: (HIGHLIGHT)

PROVOCATIVE   AMBIGUOUS   COMPLEX   EMOTIONALLY

CHALLENGING

TECHNOLOGY/ RATIONALE FOR USING IT:

PRIOR TO THE LESSON

NECESSARY BACKGROUND KNOWLEDGE/ SKILLS FOR ALL STUDENTS:

MATERIALS NEEDED:

THE LESSON: CONSTRUCT MEANING

ACTIVATE, ENGAGE AND ASSESS...

ACTIVATE AND ENGAGE LEARNER INTEREST	• ASSESS NECESSARY BACKGROUND KNOWLEDGE AND/OR SKILLS
	• SUPPLEMENT SKILLS AND BACKGROUND KNOWLEDGE

EXPLORE, DISCOVER AND DIFFERENTIATE...

	• TO DIFFERENTIATE:

SYNTHESIZE AND INTEGRATE...

REFLECT AND REVISE LESSON...

Figure 4.1.   Navigating the new pedagogy lesson planner.

CLOSING

Instruction itself is very much an art, and it is only through well-constructed and well-delivered learning experiences that students will become adept at the skills and content necessary for productive, well-rounded lives.

By Activating, Engaging, and Assessing; Exploring, Discovering, and Differentiating; and Synthesizing and Integrating, teachers create learning experiences that hook student interest, tap and assess background knowledge, gather and analyze information, and synthesize their learning into a final product. The learning becomes relevant and long lasting. Refer to Figure 4.1.

Build Relationships

> You can never teach anyone anything unless you have a relationship with them first.
>
> —Anonymous

Anyone who has had the good fortune to observe Cris Tavoni perform in a teaching lab has seen a master relationship builder at work. Tavoni is a nationally recognized expert on reading strategies. What Tavoni may do best, though, is get students over their reticence to read and analyze text, and she does this by engaging and encouraging all her students.

Tavoni places herself in the unenviable position of leading professional development in a lab setting. With educators seated along the exterior of a classroom, she leads her workshops by teaching her reading strategies to students she has never met before. She introduces herself, tells her purpose for being there, then moves in—literally. When students need help with a challenging passage, Tavoni steps right up, kneeling beside their desks to help them unearth the text's meaning.

Tavoni works shoulder-to-shoulder with students. She smiles. She laughs. She cajoles. When a struggling student offers insight into a difficult poem, she says, "You are really smart." The student's head rises. He slips off the hood on his sweatshirt and pulls his shoulders back. Her classroom lab is a positive setting, one that is educationally inspiring.

Yet Tavoni's success is intentional. To accomplish her task of teaching reading strategies, Tavoni builds positive relationships—warm, trusting relationships—and she does so within minutes.

Math teacher Rick Biggerstaff uses similar techniques in his classroom. Students often work on and solve many of their math problems in collaborative groups; they construct meaning as a team. This allows Biggerstaff to circulate among the groups to offer assistance. When students get stumped, Biggerstaff unlocks their confusion with carefully crafted questions, but not before he puts students at ease with his caring manner. Biggerstaff is extremely concerned about his students as people. He likes them, all of them, and acts in a way that results in them liking him as well. He is concerned about them as people first, young mathematicians second. This personal connection Biggerstaff makes with his students is a large reason he is so successful with students. He *endeavors* to connect with his students.

While a highly productive classroom is essential for having students meet high standards, teachers will only meet those standards by looking beyond them to something very important: the human connection. Teachers need to build bridges of positive relationships with their students. It's education's paradox. Teachers need to take time to build relationships in order to make learning time more productive.

In the crush of meeting new state and national standards, educators often forget what really motivated themselves to learn. Sure, interesting content can and should be a prime motivator, but certainly most students have had classes where friendly, engaging teachers prompted them to excel when the course was only marginally interesting to them. There, warm, caring relationships made all the difference.

Teachers who work in alternative programs designed to assist underachieving students know that strong relationships between teachers and students are key to keeping students engaged and in school. Discouraged students are fragile learners, and positive relationships keep them in classrooms.

Movies that chronicle great educational success stories in underperforming schools—*Freedom Writers* or *Stand and Deliver*, for example—illustrate how great teachers build bridges to students, and those caring, committed relationships are key to turning students around.

Yet the great void in many secondary classrooms is the nurturing atmosphere so common in elementary schools. As our students mature into young adults, teachers falsely come to believe that they function as "big people" on the inside as well. Some may become that, but most aren't. Our secondary students are sensitive individuals motivated by positive, caring relationships. When positive relations fail to exist, students turn to doing only what is asked, tuning out, or dropping out.

Needless to say, nurturing relationships need to remain appropriate and professional. Educators serve in pseudoparenting roles to our students. Yet welcoming everyone to class, acknowledging birthdays, inquiring of the downhearted, and supporting those students going through a difficult time are easily within the real and the reasonable.

While some teachers have robust, outgoing personalities, teachers need not be charismatic to be successful. They only have to play to their individual strengths. As teachers, they are trumpets and violins, flutes and drums. With the way they talk and interact, they all sound different to their students. Yet a trumpet sounds majestic and a violin tugs at the heart when played properly. Flutes can inspire lofty dreams while drums energize and unite. Teachers' varied teaching styles are very much like these instruments. They are all a different style, yet they can all inspire in their own way.

Cris Tavoni reduces the reticence to read using positive remarks, and Rick Biggerstaff unravels math's mysteries using personal connections. Each uses different strategies, yet they build solid relationships with students. As a result, students engage in learning in these warm, inviting classroom environments. These supportive relationships are the foundation upon which great learning can take place.

The Reflective Teacher

- Think back to one of your more inspiring teachers. What role did your relationship with them play in how you viewed them as exceptional educators?

CORE COVENANT

At the heart of teaching is a core proposition that impacts the entire process. This core covenant is simple: Students arrive at the beginning of the school year or term with a willingness to give the class a chance (which most students do). For their part, the teachers deliver an educational experience that is supportive, engaging, and relevant. While off-task behavior may try to derail this core covenant, the best weapon against student discipline issues are great lessons. As simple as it sounds, the best way to keep your captive-student audience captivated is through sound, engaging educational practices like those covered in this book.

This is true for both students and adults. As teachers, some of the toughest moments of classroom management arise when plodding through dry, unexciting curriculum that the *students need to know*. Those students aiming for the A do as they are dutifully asked. Other students, more questioning of the lesson's value, fidget and sometimes misbehave.

Anyone involved in professional development, though, discovers that teachers and school administrators can behave the same way. During relevant, engaging workshops, teachers and administrators are on task and courteous. They listen, participate, and ask questions. When sitting through material that is tedious and irrelevant, they tune out. Whether with students in a classroom or teachers and administrators in workshops, relevant, engaging lessons are the way to keep individuals on task.

Obviously, educators cannot control students' willingness to learn, although good relationships are critical in enhancing this. What they do control, though, is the quality of the educational product with which they engage students. Relevant, appropriately rigorous, and engaging educational experiences improve student satisfaction and result in on-task behavior; they build an intellectual bridge between teachers and students.

Quality lessons build the most important relationship in the classroom: Teacher as facilitator of learning and students as learners themselves.

GREET STUDENTS ENTHUSIASTICALLY— GET TO KNOW THEM AS INDIVIDUALS

One of education's most powerful motivational speakers, Dr. Harry Wong, emphasizes the importance of having strong relationships with students. One of Dr. Wong's suggestions is that teachers shake hands with students when they enter their classroom the first day of the term.

Whenever adults greet other adults in a professional setting, they shake hands, don't they? Try shaking hands when greeting students to a new year or semester and see what happens. Don't expect eye contact from students—in some cultures, looking elders in the eye is a sign of disrespect. Some students' grasps are limp—they find little meaning in that physical gesture.

What does surprise students and perks them up, though, is the individualized attention they receive. Seek out all students, shake their hand, greet them enthusiastically, and tell them it is a pleasure to have them in class. This is the first step to getting the semester off to a positive start.

From that day forward, find some way to greet students and welcome them (preferably by name) to your class daily. Acknowledge students outside the classroom setting as well. Whether in the hallway, in the cafeteria, or on the playground, exchange a friendly nod or smile with students. Say hello to them by name. This lets the students know that teachers care for them, that they look forward to seeing the students in class.

Adults take all kinds of cues from their supervisors and colleagues. Most would agree that a friendly "good morning" from a principal or supervisor is a great way to start a day. Even a friendly smile energizes. Students are no different.

Being on friendly, engaging terms with students is only the first step in getting to know them better. "Icebreaking" activities to start off the year or semester are essential for a glimpse into their personal lives. Some teachers assign personal crests for students to illustrate with symbols—no words are allowed. Each quadrant of the crest represents a part of their lives: favorite school activities, favorite activities outside school, family, and friends.

Students then write four short paragraphs on the back of the crest that explains the significance of the symbols. The crests are shared with the class—a document camera works well for this purpose—then posted along the walls of the classroom. A similar activity asks students to write a guided poem about their lives (each line contains requested content), and a digital photo is attached to tie the author to the literary work. In both activities, the purpose is for teachers to get to know students better so they can help and encourage them with their learning.

Getting-to-know activities do take time, but the effort spent upfront to know students better pays dividends that more that make up for the time lost in terms of positive classroom atmosphere and teacher insight into the strengths and challenges of students' lives.

These opening activities, though, are just an introduction into the journey teachers will take to know their students better. Each student enters the classroom with strengths and weaknesses in content knowledge and academic skills. Classroom activities will generate for teachers plentiful information about where students meet academic standards and where they need assistance. The attention teachers can give students to erase deficits and enhance areas of strength is really what differentiates instruction and personalizes the education system.

Yes, this is can be extremely challenging with 150 students a day at the secondary level. Yet, individualized feedback on papers and projects, quick one-on-one meetings with students to correct a misunderstanding, or personalized meetings are all tools that allow teachers to touch base with students and zero in on what they are doing correctly and where they need help to grow academically.

Teachers may rightly complain that they do not have time in their overstuffed day to make such individualized accommodations. There is no question these concerns are justified. On the other hand, what good does it do to a school system to barrel ahead with the teaching curriculum when students are falling by the wayside academically?

As discussed in Principle 4: Construct Meaning, placing students in charge of their own learning while completing an activity will keep the majority of them on task. At the same time, teachers can work with students in need of assistance either individually or in small groups. Taking time to individualize feedback and assistance is truly the only way to guarantee that all students are learning.

From the beginning, get to know the students as people as well. Find out their favorite books, sports, and hobbies—basically, their passions. Often teachers can tie content in their classrooms to aspects of students' favorite activities to explain concepts when students get confused.

Learn to read students as well. Their posture, their physical reactions, and their facial reactions are all clues to how students are reacting to activities and let teachers know to what degree they are learning. How they react to comments and suggestions will be readily readable in their body language. Frustrated countenances, furrowed brows, nods, or "I got it" all let teachers know whether or not their attempts to assist were effective.

Sometimes reactions are hard to interpret; delving into what students are thinking and feeling will allow for easier interpretation the next time that body language shows itself again. Keeping a classroom positive is essential for academic achievement, especially when the content becomes challenging. To that end, teachers should make it a goal to have a positive interaction with every student every class period (obviously, some days that may not be possible). This could mean greeting them by name as they enter, making a positive comment during a classroom discussion or activity, saying a kind word when returning a paper, or simply asking about a student's day when he or she is looking glum. When students are tardy to class, welcome them. Let them know that their presence is importance.

The truth is that many students face very challenging lives, both personally and academically. When teachers listen, they hear stories of conflicts at home or among peers. When inquiring about missing homework, students can come to tears as they open up. With very little effort, classrooms can become safe harbors from the storms in their lives.

Innumerable studies have shown the impact a caring adult can have on a kid's life. With very little effort, any teacher can be that caring adult. With individualized instruction and knowledge of students, teachers can produce wonderful academic outcomes with their students.

The Reflective Teacher

- What do I do to initiate a positive, individualized learning environment in my classroom?

BE QUIXOTIC

One of the world's great stories, Cervantes's classic *Don Quixote* became a much-loved Broadway musical whose ending draws audiences to tears. In the story, Don Quixote's mind becomes clouded by visions of chivalrous adventures. He falls in love with Aldonza, a peasant woman and prostitute, whom he calls Dulcinea. Don Quixote holds her in high regard.

Through the course of his delusional journeys, Don Quixote stirs up some trouble yet helps others out as well. Most famous is his battle with a windmill, which he sees as an invading giant. At the close of the story, though, Don Quixote is freed from his chivalrous delusions. He comes to see the world as it is. As the hero lays dying and downhearted, Aldonza forces her way into the chamber, saying that she believes in Don Quixote and will forever live her life as Dulcinea. She chooses to become the princess Don Quixote envisioned her to be.

Many excellent teachers are like Don Quixote. These teachers look into students and see the potential each contains. These teachers are the definition of quixotic: "motivated by an idealism that overlooks practical considerations."

That idealism when working with students is what separates teachers who deliver content from teachers who transform lives. Quixotic teachers make a difference by seeing the potential deep in students, and their belief in these students is often enough to lift these young people to a higher plain. They look past the negative aspects of students' lives and see the positive strengths and skills which, if nurtured, would make them successful, happy adults. Simply, they believe that talent and potential resides in each student. These teachers change lives.

These quixotic teachers are encouraging because they know that now or in the future, their words may have great impact. There is an old allegory of casting seed, acknowledging that some may fall on rock—yet also knowing that some will fall on fertile soil. Those seeds that fall on rock may not germinate. But the seeds that fall on fertile ground become lush croplands. This metaphor has powerful implications for teachers.

Educators don't always know the impact their words or gestures may have on students, yet if they continually cast positive interactions and encouragement, their efforts will find fertile soil and germinate.

The Reflective Teacher

- Look back over your life. Where has your life been changed even slightly by an encouraging word or act of faith in you?

CONTROL VS. RESPECT

There was once a saying in secondary education that went, "Never smile until October." The thinking was that if teachers remained stern, students would know they meant business, get to work, and stay under control. Anyone who has ever allowed a class to get out of hand knows that it is easier to loosen up than tighten up.

The concept of what an appropriate classroom looks like, though, is evolving. At one time, strict classroom management was paramount. Administrators wanted quiet classrooms where teens were studiously at work. To accomplish this, teachers needed to keep a pretty tight rein on their students. To maintain this classroom control, progressive discipline was established that went somewhat like this: The first offense for disruption was dealt a warning. Additional offenses resulted in after-school detention. Beyond that, teaches referred students to the vice principal for further discipline.

While this may remain an effective way of maintaining classroom discipline, strict, controlling classroom environments run contrary to good, collaborative instructional practices. Tight rules will not create the collaborative environments necessary for using the principles found in this book; only respect will.

One teacher explained that his transformation away from a classroom focusing on control and toward one emphasizing respect came about five years into his teaching career. The teacher had a disruptive freshman student named Mike. The student's arrogance (as the teacher perceived it) rubbed him the wrong way. This young teen was quite bright, but his defiant talking during discussions and his disruptive behavior while working in groups had become tiresome.

One day, the teacher had had enough of Mike's insolence and confronted him in front of his classmates. Blasted by the teacher's storm of pent-up anger, Mike quieted, but the teacher's actions were very unsettling to himself. He returned to his desk and thought, "Would I like it if my principal had ripped me in front of my peers during a staff meeting?"

Believing that he should treat his students like he would like to be treated, the teacher halted all class activities, hushed the students, and apologized to Mike in front of everyone for his outburst. He then extended his hand, and Mike shook it. The teacher did it for his own peace of mind, but the result surprised him. From that moment forward, Mike became a hardworking, respectful, and model student.

As a result of seeing this, the teacher decided to treat his students in the same respectful, friendly way that he would like to be treated. Rather than control, he really worked to build mutual respect. If he needed to confront a student, he would do so after school or between periods. The teacher lived by the saying: Criticize in private, compliment in public. The easiest way to greatly reduce classroom misbehavior is to do the following:

- Get students engaged in interesting, relevant lessons (using the principles discussed in this book).
- Create a learning environment built on rapport and respect. This classroom should be warm and supportive, although intolerant of behavior that runs contrary to a positive learning environment. Building this style of classroom environment takes longer to establish than one based on a strict, controlling policy—but in the long run, students become self-managers of their behavior.

This is a simple formula. For most students, it works.

STRESS AND LEARNING

Many feel it when traffic slows to a crawl, and they may be late to an early-morning staff meeting. It can intensify at night when worries keep people from sound sleep. The National Geographic special "Stress: Portrait of a Killer" outlines multiple ways that stress not only shortens lives, it impacts the degree to which people learn.[1] The special highlights the work of Stanford University's professor of neuroscience Dr. Robert Sapolsky's work. His research on wild baboons identified parallels that exist between their species and humans.

When Sapolsky first began studying these primates in Africa decades ago, he observed a pack tightly controlled by alpha males which led by intimidation and attack. A recipient of a MacArthur "genius" fellowship, Sapolsky studied the impacts of overt control on the health of both the alpha males and the oppressed baboons and found physiological evidence that this stress produced killer responses like high blood pressure, reduced immune systems, and poorer health.

The National Geographic special then drew parallels with studies of British civil servants and found that hierarchical, oppressive social settings produced the same response in humans. What also was shown in the special, though, was how stress can negatively impact the memory—think high-stakes tests here—and how incessant bouts of stress can actually unravel the brain's ability to remember.

For Sapolsky, though, what appeared at first to be a tragic end to his studies turned out to be a turning point. Years into his study, his pack of baboons stumbled upon trash from a tourist lodge where meat tainted with tuberculosis infected the primates. Sapolsky was crushed, thinking that all his research would come to an end.

What happened, though, proved enlightening and valuable. Of the baboons that fell ill, only the aggressive alpha males died. Eventually, rising to take their place were more nurturing males, taught to be gentle by the females in the pack. Rather than using the opportunity to gain control and continue the pattern of ruling through fear, the kinder male baboons were nurturing. As a result of gentler treatment, killer stress symptoms abated, and all baboons became healthier. Further, when headstrong alpha males joined the pack later, they were taught the gentler ways and gave up their aggressive behavior.

While unavoidable high-stakes tests can certainly produce anxieties, classrooms themselves should not be environments where aggressive measures by alpha teachers (or bullying students) control student behavior. While it may provide for a controlled and structured environment, the stress this aggressive climate brings impacts student learning negatively.

Classroom management through force may breed submissive students, but teachers must never confuse compliance with buy in. Students in these classrooms do what they need to do to get the grade and get out, or they opt not to buy in at all and simply fail.

There is a better way to maintain appropriate classroom discipline.

The Reflective Teacher

- What kind of environment do I create in my classroom? One built upon control? Or one based upon nurturing and mutual respect?

DISCIPLINE STEALTHILY

No matter what relationship teachers build with their students, inappropriate behavior will occur in a classroom. What is the best way to handle it? If it is isolated, not calling attention to it is the first step.

Take, for example, an instance where a teacher is giving instructions and a student is talking to her neighbors when she should be paying attention. (In reality, this happens regularly, doesn't it?) Two responses are possible. The first is disruptive: The teacher stops giving instructions and confronts the student in front of her peers. All attention fades from the lesson and focuses on the offending student. If a student is seeking attention, this is a sure way for a teacher to give it to her.

An alternative method keeps the focus on the lesson and away from the student. Call this the "surgical strike," a military term for a precise attack. In this method, the teacher catches the offending student's eye then beams a laserlike glare the student's way. If that doesn't work, the teacher, while continuing with his or her teaching, strolls alongside the student and stands there. The vast majority of the time, this is enough. The instruction continues uninterrupted. The student's behavior is directed toward learning.

The same applies if a student is off task. Merely stroll next to the student. If that doesn't work, point to the task on the desk or computer that must be completed. When the student acknowledges, smile. Thank them softly.

Classroom management—which is creating and maintaining a classroom environment appropriate for student learning—is essential for instruction. Nonverbal solutions are the best first strike when discipline issues arise. A firm get-to-business glare is a great tool when it is followed by a smile when good behavior resumes. Redirecting with a "surgical strike" rather than reprimanding verbally maintains the learning environment but also builds rapport and trust because it limits embarrassment.

On occasion, a more firm approach is needed. If the disruptions continue, ask the student to remain after class. If the behavior is extremely disruptive or disrespectful, request that the student leave the classroom and go to the hallway. In either case, keep any negative interactions invisible from the student's peers. Protect the student's self-esteem. Solid expectations for good behavior and respectful treatment are recipes for respect.

Classroom management is a complex topic worthy of books and workshops. Not all disruptive behavior can be solved by these simple approaches—but a majority will. The more respectful the teacher's efforts to keep students on task, the fewer discipline problems there will be.

No adult likes to be humiliated or reprimanded. Why would students? Be firm but respectful and students will repay it with better, on-task behavior. Everyone works harder for those who like them and treat them with respect. Create that kind of learning environment in classrooms. By treating students in a respectful manner when they get out of line, teachers are protecting the students' self-esteem and building a better relationship with them.

The Reflective Teacher

- What respectful methods do I employ when I need to redirect students who are off task?

DON'T SNUFF THE FIRE

One of the great mysteries of education is why youngsters' love for learning so often diminishes when they move to secondary school and become teenagers. Anyone who has raised teenagers knows that this volatile passage through life is one of shifting priorities. Yet the question remains: How can students who soak up learning in elementary school, for example, become young adults who grow to have little interest in learning in high school?

Many parents witness this change in their sons and daughters. Their kids have nurturing elementary teachers. Their sons and daughters are hardworking kids, at that stage, who look forward to going to school. By freshman year of high school, though, their relationship with school changes. The classes they enjoy the most and work hardest in are the classes where they *like* their teachers. In the other classes, they do the work to get the grade—but there is often little joy there.

Not surprisingly, their favorite teachers are often educators who purposefully create nurturing environments in their classrooms. These teachers create rapport with their students. Their classrooms are encouraging learning environments. So how do teachers go about showing that they care about their students?

TREAT STUDENTS LIKE CUSTOMERS

As a patron of stores, hotels, and restaurants, every teacher has received varied levels of customer service. Poor service may elicit a conversation with a manager; most often, though, most people respond by not returning to the establishment. Excellent service fills customers with a sense that their patronage is appreciated. They feel wanted and want to return.

Should classrooms be any different? As teachers, it is easy to fall into the habit of taking students for granted. Educators have somewhat of a guarantee: There will always be more children. In this profession, teachers with enough seniority can feel secure. They lay down classroom rules and expect the students to comply.

Struggling under tremendous workloads, teachers may groan when new students enter their class or secretly rejoice when problem students transfer to another class or school. It is easy to fall into the mode of creating lessons, teaching students, and handing back papers in a routine that can become pretty mechanical.

The most effective teachers, though, treat students as individuals worthy of their best treatment—not as guaranteed customers of their service. They treat student as if they had the option to go elsewhere if their teaching performance is not up to par.

The heart of the charter-school concept is this idea that students ought to have a choice of where to learn, just as teachers, as consumers, can choose where to shop, eat, and stay. Many school districts have implemented a school-choice option, whereby students can transfer to the school of their choice; but what if students were allowed to shop for their teachers as well?

Students who feel like valued customers tend to act like they are valued. They work harder. They behave better. They are friendlier. An ethic of customer service in the classroom is a productive way to function.

The Reflective Teacher

- How do I regularly show students that they are valued in my classroom?

BUILD STUDENT-TO-STUDENT RELATIONSHIPS

Teachers would like to believe that students' primary reason for coming to school is to learn. For many that may be the case. Often, though, the learning component is only part of a student's day. Along with learning, students come to school to see friends and interact with peers. The evidence of this is very apparent. Students scoot class to class, cell phones in hand. Chances are, students aren't texting their friends about academic issues.

Equally true is the reluctance of students to engage in learning when they lack friends in school or have conflicts with peers. Effective teachers, therefore, work to make their classroom a healthy environment where students not only treat their peers with respect, they have the opportunity to build friendships as well.

Seating charts and desk configurations are one easy way to build relationships. Rather than straight, sterile rows that isolate students, teachers can arrange desks into groups so that students get to know one another through collaborative work.

When given the option of seating choices, students often opt to sit with their friends. If they want to limit their interaction with the teacher, they try to sit in the back row. While this can make students feel comfortable, veteran teachers know that this often is an attempt to keep from interacting.

Mixing up students can create a more focused learning environment. This also allows new relationships to be made. Old friendships are not lost; students can still comingle before or at the end of class. Students who may normally duck for the cover of the back row are brought into the fold. Students get to know classmates that they might not get acquainted with if they had their choice of seating.

When creating seating charts, teachers can run extra copies of desk configurations and have students fill out ones for themselves. Expecting students to know each others' names is a first step toward tearing down the barriers between them. Changing seating arrangements every month or two allows students to get to know and work with other students.

Explore and Discover learning environments, like those discussed in this book, have the advantage of building positive relationships as well. Socratic seminars and Nun Thing discussions get students talking to one another face-to-face. Small-group analysis gets students talking and knowing one another better. Normally quiet students are nudged into participating. Performance tasks place students in groupings where they need to work together and get to know one another better.

Activities as simple as peer editing, where students conference over written work, give students the opportunity to know one another better if the groups are arranged intentionally. Discussion techniques like "think pair share" require two students to conference over a topic before they explain their ideas to the large group. This teamwork builds relationships among former strangers.

Rallying students around a theme is a great way to create a positive group identity. One secondary school states, "It takes a little more to be a Tiger," which is its mascot. The statement not only helps create high expectations for students, it also creates a sense of group identity, where all students are encouraged to join. Warm, respectful relationships, intentionally created, not only make the classroom a more conducive learning environment, they make it a much more inviting place to be as well.

In the era of heavy reliance among teens on social-networking Internet sites to communicate and interact, creating relationships through face-to-face interaction with peers is a skill that needs to be fostered.

BUILD BRIDGES TO FAMILIES AND GUARDIANS

Unfortunately, it seems that the connections between parents and schools slowly erode as students move from elementary through secondary school and on to high school. The reasons for this are obvious but not often addressed.

Students go from having one teacher all day in elementary school to six or more on their secondary-school schedule. Parents go from twice-a-year elementary parent-teacher conferences, where a child's performance and conduct is discussed, to a once-a-year open house, which can be largely a 15-minute spiel per class about how the semester will go. Parental volunteerism can be common in elementary classrooms. Parental presence in secondary classrooms is largely nonexistent.

Not surprisingly, students appear to be more successful across the board in the elementary grades. Entering high school is a major bump in the road. Drop-out rates peak during freshman and sophomore years.

Can the academic and social problems students face at the secondary level be blamed on the disconnect that grows between families and schools? Perhaps, to some extent. Certainly, the rush of hormones and the push for independence teenagers experience make teaching secondary students a daunting task. Yet parents and guardians are valuable allies in this effort.

Too often secondary teachers believe that their responsibility ends when they post grades online or send (or e-mail) progress reports home. The assumption is that parents or guardians receive the grade reports then congratulate their students on good grades or discuss ways to boost scores. Basically, the teachers have done their part. It is now time for parents to do theirs. In many homes, this is the case. However, in homes where parents do not understand academic success and are reluctant to contact teachers with questions or concerns, the students suffer.

While it is expected in a standards-based environment that most students will start below standard at the beginning of the course, parents and guardians of students not making regular progress toward course expectations should be contacted.

Contact with parents or guardians can be vital to student growth. Hours can be spent calling parents at home or at work—but the results can be remarkable. Teachers can slash their students' poor performance rate by making calls to parents outlining students' positive progress and where they needed to apply effort to achieve a stronger score.

No matter the student's progress or lack of progress in a class, teachers should always make it a point to say positive things about him or her. Rarely is academic failure isolated. Often, students who struggle in one class, struggle in other classes as well. Parents can become exasperated with their son or daughter. Talking up students' positive traits calms parents and places the academic problems into a proper focus.

When time allows, call parents whose students are high achievers in class, as well. The calls often surprise parents, but they become delighted to receive a call filled with good news. Phone calls are the best way of making allies of parents or guardians. Once rapport is established, e-mail can be an effective tool to communicate quickly and easily about student progress, but it is best to establish a relationship first through talking either on the phone or face- to-face.

Perhaps one of the biggest challenges of the educational community is building connections with parents who feel disenfranchised from the school system. Some parents may have had poor educational experiences, and they feel reticent about entering schools. Other parents may be immigrants to this country and feel out of place due to language barriers. Still others may simply be intimidated by educational institutions.

While educators ideally would like schools to be the gathering places in their communities where all feel welcome, the reality is that underperforming schools are often disconnected from their community. They are places where students struggle, stumble, and suffer. Yet schools that work to turn failure to success also realize the need to reach out to the community and invite parents and guardians in.

Probably the simplest way to accomplish this is through parent conferences that extend to the upper grades. While twice-yearly conferences in the elementary grades are the norm in most districts, secondary schools are beginning to establish the practice as well. In these districts, student-led conferences are proving to be successful ways to reconnect parents and guardians. Conferences are organized through a homeroom or advisory class. Portfolios of work and progress reports for all classes are assembled, and the students lead the discussion about their academic progress.

While parents may not meet face-to-face with their child's individual teachers, they do get a report about growth and areas of needed improvement from the person who matters most: their students. Follow-up conferences with specific teachers can be scheduled.

Schools that organize after-school community-building activities find them an effective way to engage parents. Garfield Elementary, a school with close to 70 percent of students on free or reduced-price lunches, has been very proactive in its outreach to its community. In the fall, the school hosts its game night, where students and their parents are invited for a Friday night of activities.

Prior to the winter break, families are invited to its Snowflake Social. Lunch tables in the gym are filled with holiday gifts ranging in price from 50 cents to $10 for students to purchase and gift wrap (a fund is set up for students who can't afford them). From the gift tables, students move into the cafeteria, where they go station-to-station creating a variety of holiday cards. Parents and guardians are invited. Hot drinks and snacks are served.

Scheduled in the spring, Garfield's Multicultural Night presents a variety of food, hands-on cultural displays, and arts and crafts. Not by accident, the cultures represented on Multicultural Night mirror the eclectic mix of the school's student body. The end-of-the-year Literacy Fair celebrates a school year of hard work for students. There are tables and displays of students' work, and parents and district staff are invited. (In the area of literacy, Garfield's state test scores perform at levels similar to the city's more affluent schools—no surprise, given the enthusiastic support for reading and writing.)

Activities such as these break down barriers that separate parents and guardians from the schools their children attend. As a result, the parents become supporters of the education their children are receiving.

Good teachers want all students to succeed. To accomplish this goal, they go out of their way to enlist the support of parents and guardians whenever possible.

The Reflective Teacher

- What connections do I intentionally make with the parents or guardians of my students?
- How do I leverage parent support to improve student learning in my classroom?

BUILD CONNECTIONS TO COLLEAGUES—COLLABORATE

Teachers with a few decades of experience can attest to the fact that education was for many years a lonely profession. Teachers had their grade-level or department meetings. They'd gather to iron out unit timetables or schedule book usage. The discussions usually covered the nuts and bolts (and complaints) of their duties, the conversations usually being limited to content knowledge.

Teachers had great ideas, but there wasn't an *ethic* that led people to share or discuss them. Basically, teachers left the meetings, entered their classrooms, and closed the doors behind themselves. Teachers were contractors with a job to do. Only the younger, inexperienced teachers asked for help.

Today, state-mandated assessments reveal scores broken down by school, grade level, classroom, and skill. The push—rightly so—is to give each student the best education possible—and the student's progress toward these standards is stored electronically. As a result, the challenges facing education are bigger than any one teacher can solve; only through teamwork can schools raise their teaching to the standards required by their state. In short, if "two heads are better than one," as the saying goes, more eyes on a problem will most likely lead to better outcomes.

Teachers need to collaborate to solve their school's educational issues. Collaboration is not the following: meetings where teachers sit passively and only listen. Collaboration should not feel like drudgery.

Collaboration should be *active and creative*. Its intent should be to solve problems. In collaboration, teachers function like a team. They discuss and possibly debate best teaching practices. They delve into what they plan to do to improve instruction and how they expect to measure outcomes. Afterwards, they delve into *what* they saw when classroom practices were working effectively and *why* they worked— or what they saw when outcomes fell short and what could be changed to improve them. Student progress is paramount. In collaboration meetings, teachers bring work samples of struggling students and look to their group for suggestions. In the end, good collaboration creates *better understanding*.

While collaborative sessions can be demanding, the work should be uplifting and the outcome rewarding. It is exciting to think about effective teaching practices and their impact on student learning. Teachers deeply steeped in a collaborative culture come to wonder how they would function without the support and feedback of their fellow educators.

Often, the first step in building good collaborative teams it to come to agreement on what will be the norms for the meetings. Sometimes, the lion's share of the first meeting will be spent deciding the group's norms of behavior. A draft of the norms is written and revised as is necessary at the meetings that follow. Common norms for collaborative groups are as follows:

- Assume positive intent in people's actions and ideas.
- Ensure that everyone has the opportunity to share ideas.
- Work to achieve consensus. Vote on a proposal either to affirm consensus or when a stalemate has occurred.
- Create an environment where people feel free to share. What is reported in confidence should not be repeated outside the meeting.
- Turn cell phones off during the meeting.

In the educational setting, the focus of collaboration should be on improving teaching and education. Educators in Japan view teaching as an art that can be improved through collaboration and revision. In Japanese Lesson Study, groups of teachers collaboratively create a lesson as a team. Next, one member of the group teaches the lesson in his or her classroom while the rest observe.

In Lesson Study, though, most of the attention is focused on the students during the lesson, and the observing teachers roam among the desks taking notes on the task at hand and asking clarifying questions of the students, if needed. Again, the focus is on how the lesson impacts the students. Are students engaged in the lesson? Are there elements that they find confusing? Are the final outcomes as rich as was hoped for?

With observations and notes gathered, the cohort reconvenes for a rich discussion of the lesson. Every member reflects on how the lesson went. Since all members helped create the lesson, each has a stake in its improvement. There is no finger pointing. All are interested in bettering the final results. The discussion of lesson improvements becomes a learning experience for this group of professionals. Based on the group's reflective feedback, the lesson is revised and eventually taught to a different group of students.

Lesson Study in this collaborative format has had profound impact on American teachers who have practiced versions of it. During lesson-planning sessions, teachers get deeply engaged in understanding the state standards that apply to lessons. Discussions are deep and earnest regarding the big idea or ideas to be taught. Teachers work as teams to make their lessons engaging for the students. During the lesson-observation phase, teachers embed themselves among the students. Student engagement, performance, and distraction are assessed. Afterwards, earnest problem-solving sessions lead to improvements.

For all its benefits, there is nothing mystical about a Lesson Study–style approach to lesson development and improvement. The collaborative process brings a structured approach to problem solving: how to develop a lesson, judge its effectiveness based on student performance, revise it, and teach it again—with more revisions to come.

Collaboration is a powerful tool to create curriculum and test it as objectively as possible in the only laboratory where it counts: the classroom. Reflection on student engagement and achievement leads to revisions that push efforts forward to improve classroom practice.

The camaraderie that collaboration builds among professionals, though, may be as valuable as any single part of the process. Separated into classrooms, teachers often lead isolated professional existences. True collaboration—that is, teamwork collaboration not "staff-meeting" collaboration—can be a rejuvenating experience in a profession that requires tremendous amounts of energy.

Collaborative discussion about standards, big ideas, effective teaching practices and strategies to help struggling learners improve classroom practices and build unity among grade-level teams. In extreme cases, departments separated by differences have been reunited by collaborating around a common purpose.

Teaching and learning are far too complex a process for educators to go it alone. The challenges are too great for anyone to solve individually. By collaborating, teachers not only improve the educational process, they build relationships between themselves and their colleagues that are both productive and rejuvenating.

The Reflective Teacher

- How do I regularly work with my colleagues for the purpose of improving instructional practice? How do I rely upon them for emotional support?

CLOSING

The new three Rs in education—rigor, relevance, and relationships—place human interaction as a top priority. Highly effective teachers are rarely those who "don't smile' for the first month of school. They are teachers who joyfully introduce themselves to students at the beginning of the term. They are friendly, supportive, and respectful throughout the school year. These teachers are effective with their students because they earn their respect. There is laughter in their classrooms. Students are on task and productive. Students learn because the teachers are attentive to individual needs and skill levels—and they work with students individually to help them grow.

Likewise, it is important for teachers to build relationships with parents and guardians—powerful allies in the teaching process. Due to the profession's demands and complexity, educators need to collaborate with one another to improve curriculum and teaching practice. In the end, teachers through their relationships have dramatic power to influence those around them.

The following, attributed to German poet Goethe, makes a striking statement about the power of the individual to impact those around them:

> I have come to the frightening conclusion that I am the decisive element. It is my personal approach that creates the climate. It is my daily mood that makes the weather. I possess tremendous power to make life miserable or joyous. I can be a tool of torture or an instrument of inspiration. I can humiliate or humor, hurt or heal. In all situations, it is my response that decides whether a crisis is escalated or de-escalated, and a person is humanized or de-humanized. If we treat people as they are, we make them worse. If we treat people as they ought to be, we help them become what they are capable of becoming.

While Goethe's words certainly inspire a proactive approach to life, his insight certainly applies to the classroom. While students are "our customers" and the focus of the work, teachers themselves are the single most important person in their classroom because they control so many of the factors that contribute to student success. It is teachers' actions and their attitudes that to a large degree create partnerships with parents and positive professional relationships with colleagues. Likewise, schools and teachers can invite parents in and make them partners in their child's education.

Teachers can build the finest lessons and employ the best teaching practices—but by building relationships, they dramatically improve success in their classrooms.

Honor Individuality

Thomas Edison, Bill Gates, Rachel Carson, Rosa Parks—each of these individuals radically changed the world landscape. From lightbulbs to computers, and a healthy environment to personal freedoms, single individuals were key to making these transformations take place.

Agreed, few ever attain greatness in isolation; outstanding accomplishments are realized with the help of others, and this is certainly true of the innovators mentioned above. Yet at one time, these individuals who drove scientific and social change sat in classrooms. They were youngsters and teenagers, not unlike the ones roaming school hallways today.

It is hard to tell what innovative technology, medical breakthrough, or social change will transform the world next. But one thing is clear: The individuals who will accomplish these great feats are today's students. Educators need to arm them with the skills and processes necessary for them to accomplish their aspirations.

Society needs productive, well-rounded, and well-balanced individuals leaving schools. Yet more than that, schools need to produce creative, imaginative individuals—innovators—whose contributions to society will change the way society lives. To accomplish this, schools must nurture students by honoring their individuality.

Lodged within students are dreams and aspirations for their futures. In each lies the potential to make a meaningful contribution to the world. How do teachers go about educating students to their own potentialities, rather than just to some generic norm the system holds for them? How do educators individualize instruction and strive to make our students the determiners of their destiny?

The answer is both simple and complex: Teachers create ways for students to excel in their areas of strength, while finding methods to help them build the skills and knowledge necessary to function highly as adults.

GIVE STUDENTS CHOICES

At its heart, the student-centered classroom honors the individuality of its students. Rather than being forced into one central track, students should be urged to take side channels of their choice to explore areas of interest to them. What ties these varied activities or strands of units of study together are common standards that all students must meet.

First off, teachers can start by giving students a diverse curriculum that promotes rich thinking. The old-school method of teaching school relied upon a single source of information (the textbook) and study guides to be completed. If ecologists were to look at this teaching strategy, they would call this monoculture: a landscape devoid of diversity. Living in an information-rich era, cumbersome textbooks are giving way to a variety of electronic resources or shorter texts that have a better chance of engaging students with their diverse information and opinions. Offering students choices increases their chances of them becoming hooked on the content.

Honoring individuality is a solid step toward improving literacy. Reading experts tell teachers that one of the best ways to get students reading—and thus improve their reading skills—is to give them choice in what they want to read.

Literature or social-studies classes typically assign whole-class reading of a common work. If students are capable of reading the required selection and enjoy it, they may complete the reading. If they aren't engaged in the assignment, they may fudge their answers from an online source. In many cases, forced selections sends students scrambling to get the assignment completed with as little reading as possible. Choice changes this scenario.

When students get to choose a reading selection of interest and appropriate challenge (students need to be trained to identify books of appropriate difficulty), they become more engaged in their reading. This, of course, requires teachers to do extra work identifying titles that would meet the course or unit standards, but students who have five books from which to choose have a much better chance of becoming engaged in their reading than those who have one choice forced upon them, which in fact may be too challenging or easy for them, not to mention of little interest.

Likewise, mathematics can be made more interesting by giving students choices of problems to solve. Rather than one problem for the class to solve, multiple problems can be offered. For example, one of the most confusing parts of being a consumer is figuring out which product is truly the best deal. A consumer purchases a washing machine at a bargain, but due to its less efficient design, it may end up costing more after three years of service than an efficient, more expensive model.

Which car to purchase, which cell-phone provider to choose from, which college to attend (when you add in all related costs)—all these are real-world problems that can be solved by common mathematical concepts. Rather than assign one problem to the class, the teacher, to increase student engagement, gives multiple scenarios—and allows students to solve their own relevant problems if the one they suggest requires application of the mathematical concepts under study. The students' individuality is honored by allowing them to pursue the study of a topic of interest and relevance to themselves.

Similarly, in social studies, choice can be given in the study of a given concept. Take, for example, the idea of the "cause" of the American Revolution. Rather than skimming the impact of the French and Indian War, the Stamp Act, the Boston Massacre, etc., to identify causes for America's separation from England, teachers can offer students the choice of analyzing one event in detail (these make excellent group activities).

Examining one event of interest, students look in-depth at the historical forces at work. To conclude this unit, students report their findings to the rest of the class—thus rounding out the learning experience for all.

The standards for success for this social-studies assignment, for example, would be based on a rubric that outlined the depth of analysis, the quality of the cause-effect connection, and the thoroughness of the details and examples in the final project or presentation.

Again, student choice is honored—learning is defined and assessed through the common skills and concepts necessary to complete the task. Further, the skills necessary to meet standards for this project should align with those necessary to complete research on an adult task, making this a relevant learning activity.

To honor the individuality of their students, teachers need to create as much diversity as possible in their reading selections and assignments, using engagement and relevance as the bellwether for their decision making.

Similarly, giving choice in final performance tasks vastly increases the odds of getting excellent projects turned in. A variety of tasks should be offered (with students having the option to propose their own), and a variety of presentation options should be permitted. From cell phones to the Internet to social-networking sites, students today are immersed in a technology-rich world. Using technology as a platform for a final project gives the students the opportunity for creativity and personal expression.

Where once poster board was the standard canvas for academic expression, today electronic presentation devices like websites, PowerPoint, Photo Story, digital cameras (both video and still), and easy-to-use video software allow unparalleled personal expression. Give students clear performance tasks, models that define success and articulate rubrics, and student creativity and personal expression flourish. Such projects prompt a very creative form of thinking and individual expression.

Further, simple technology like document cameras allow students to share and celebrate their work. Having students project their work for the class to see is a great way of honoring their efforts and can be an excellent source for suggestions.

The Reflective Teacher

- How can I create or modify assignments and projects to honor varied interests and, as a result, increase the level of engagement and relevance?

HONOR STUDENTS' DIVERSE LIVES AND CULTURES

As much as any time in the past, teachers are dealing with diverse socioeconomic student populations. Honoring individuality means knowing students' background and respecting cultural differences. Giving students the opportunity to share their culture and varied backgrounds not only improves engagement in projects and activities, it proves to be a good learning experience for other classmates.

As much as teachers may have trouble admitting it, students have lives and activities going on outside the classroom that may be as important to their growth as individuals as what they learn in an academic setting. Sports, drama club, and debate all build necessary life skills. So do after-school jobs.

The time required of these activities, though, can sometimes conflict with school assignments. When teachers hold to inflexible deadlines, students may opt to not complete their schoolwork—and the student suffers. While it is certainly important for students to learn the importance of timeliness, occasional flexibility on the part of teachers allows students to excel on more than one front.

Students are also multifaceted in their academic strengths and weaknesses. Students who sail through science and math classes may struggle in less quantitative subjects such as English and social studies—and the reverse is true as well. For some students, meeting a standard in a subject area is an accomplishment—and this should be celebrated.

No matter what class students are attending at the time, teachers should encourage students to pursue their areas of talents and passion, whether this be calculus, chemistry, or car repair. By focusing and celebrating student success, teachers help direct them toward satisfying careers.

The Reflective Teacher

- How do the activities I create allow students to celebrate their diverse backgrounds?

HONOR INDIVIDUALITY BY DIFFERENTIATING INSTRUCTION

At any given time in a classroom, some students are on target to meet the curriculum standard, some have met it, and some are still emerging in their skills or content knowledge. No two students in a classroom are in precisely the same place in their learning.

If teachers are truly to honor individuality, they need to honor nonjudgmentally the fact that students will learn and master concepts and skills at different rates. To be shy on conceptual knowledge or short on skills may not be the fault of the student; it may be the result of their previous learning environment. Likewise, to be slow to grasp a concept has no reflection on whether or not the student will eventually meet curriculum standards.

Students are individuals, each with diverse academic strengths and areas that need attention. In order to respond to these differences in learning, teachers must differentiate instruction based on students' needs if they are to help all students grow academically. One lesson taught at one speed will not foster growth for all students in an academically diverse classroom.

The change from a "group-teach" mentality to a differentiated classroom represents a fundamental shift in teaching philosophy and classroom practice. It represents a shift away from the assembly-line approach—where all students are taught at one speed—to a more custom-built philosophy, where students are viewed as individuals with a range of skill and abilities to address.

The assembly-line approach to teaching does not honor individuality. Students receive one learning experience, and this learning activity is meant to suffice. With a well-crafted lesson, the majority of students may learn; those that don't, though, are often left behind to try to learn on their own while the class moves ahead. Or worse, the teacher accepts it as inevitable that some will be left behind. When students are grouped in classes on a homogeneous basis (like an honors or AP course), this approach may suffice at times.

Where the assembly-line approach falls short, though, is in classrooms with a wide range of skills and foundational knowledge. Educators try to "teach to the middle," thus leaving both high and low students short on their learning if no further assistance is provided.

Certainly the thought of "individualizing instruction" with a full class of rambunctious elementary kids or five sections of secondary students could seem overwhelming at first, but look at how this might be done in large-group golf lessons. Anyone who has taken a group golf lesson has experienced differentiated instruction.

As the group forms for the first lesson, the golf pro takes the new players to the driving range, teaches them the basics of hitting the ball, then sets them to work practicing. Some students most likely have had golf experience, so they make decent drives immediately. Other new players have mixed results: some hit the ball a few dozen yards; others barely swat it off the tee.

Rather than leaving his students to practice and returning to the clubhouse to finish balancing his accounts (the equivalent of one-lesson-taught/some-students-will-fail ethic), the pro circulates among his students. He watches their swings, diagnoses their errors, and makes a pointer or two to improve their performance.

If a number of golfers are experiencing the same errors, the pro groups them together. Rather than make the same suggestion again and again, he finds it more efficient to teach the concept in a group setting while the rest of his class continues with their activities.

No golf pro expects a group of new golfers to have the same range or skills. No pro expects his golf students to learn at the same rate. The adept golf pro both teaches the group and instructs individuals in the same session. The golf pro honors individuality.

At its heart, differentiated instruction in a classroom works the same way. The teacher gets the class working on a learning activity where students are engaged either individually or in collaborative groups. (Review how this is addressed in Principle 4: Construct Learning.) This frees the teacher to observe student work, diagnose potential difficulties, and work with students one-on-one or in small groups while the rest of the class continues with the activity.

If necessary, students in need of help can meet with the teacher before or after school, but given students' busy lives, differentiation during class time can be the most productive. Running concurrent learning experiences takes some practice, but with time, it can become second nature.

Essential to effective differentiation is organization of student data. Grade books organized around essential skills and content knowledge (as opposed to a list of jumbled scores running chronologically) allow the teacher an easy-to-read, individualized glimpse of students' academic performance. For example, if a group of students received "below-standard" scores for "Ideas and Organization" on their last essay, the teacher could group these students together to work on this skill while the rest of the class begins their prewrite activity for their next essay.

In a science class, the teacher might circulate among students involved in a discovery activity, looking at results, asking clarifying questions, and redirecting students who had low scores on a similar concept on the last assessment. If necessary, the science teacher could group students together if a number of them need the same assistance. In either example, the teacher is differentiating instruction based on academic needs.

Differentiated instruction also may result in a shift in assessment priorities. Rather than spend large amounts of time after school hours grading student work, this differentiated model calls for feedback to be given during class, face-to-face with students.

In no way can the importance of this kind of interaction be underestimated. When teachers purposefully take time to work with students one-on-one or in groups, they are honoring their individuality and showing that each student has value. Students connect to these teachers, listen to their suggestions, and, because they have been actively involved, take more ownership in their learning.

Classrooms are filled with individuals who vary in their areas of strength and need. Teachers who differentiate their instruction honor the individuality of these students.

The Reflective Teacher

- How does my classroom practice ensure that all students get the help they need?

GRADE-HONORING INDIVIDUALITY

Everyone learns at different rates. If the scope and sequence of lessons are appropriate, most students should be able to perform at course standards by the end of a given unit. For some, though, the skills and understanding may still be "emerging" when a unit comes to a conclusion. If an indelible grade is given, this summative assessment follows students through their academic career.

What if the grading system were more flexible? What if a student "gets" a concept or can perform a vital skill after a unit is over? Should students be able to go back and challenge a score after a unit is completed, as long as they do so within a reasonable timeframe (the grading period, for example)?

If teachers want to honor individuality and assess students' abilities, they need to give students every opportunity to show their best effort. This is a core component of standards-based grading. Rather than averaging scores over the course of the year—mixing September's and January's scores—teachers should assess in ways that identify the students' end-of-the-term skill levels.

Student skill levels and conceptual knowledge should be assessed at their strongest point—even if this comes after a unit is completed. For example, if a student doesn't display an adequate understanding of some vital concept in an earth-science unit but, due to related learning, displays adequate knowledge later in the course, the score for the final level of understanding should overwrite the grade given *during* the unit.

Again, assessment at this depth requires a carefully organized grade book and a belief that learning, whenever it happens, should be honored. By allowing flexibility, though, students are recognized for what they came to finally understand within the semester or trimester. This more open-ended means of assessment allows students to grow through the end of the grading period.

As Carol Ann Tomlinson and Jay McTighe state in *Integrating Differentiated Instruction and Understanding by Design*, "A grade should give as clear a measure as possible of the best a student can do."[1]

An open, knowable, flexible grading system makes students the determiners of their future and encourages them to continue working hard to succeed. The old method of averaging grades really discourages student effort: Why work hard when old scores will drag them down, students wonder? Assessing scores on best efforts (truly summative assessments of growth) encourages students to work harder through a grading period and honors them as individuals since everyone learns at different rates.

The Reflective Teacher

- How can I make my grading system more flexible to encourage students to meet course standards within the grading period?

PROMPT STUDENTS TOWARD THEIR FUTURE

Creating classroom environments where students ponder their future honors their individual paths in life. If school is anything, it should be preparation for the individual futures that students dream of. When curriculum allows for students to ponder what's ahead for them as individuals, the results can be impressive.

Washington State, for example, requires for graduation an in-depth "culminating project" in students' senior year of high school. The purpose of the culminating project is to take skills learned in school and apply them to an area of interest. This may be the exploration of a future career or growth in some facet as an individual.

The culminating project requires the step-by-step completion of a variety of activities with real-world application: a business-style proposal letter, in-depth research on a future career or hobby of interest, a research paper synthesizing the results, and 20 hours of work on the project. For the final step, students must give a presentation to a group of adults.

What is most impressive when viewing these presentations is the energy and interest students pour into exploring a future career or a hobby of interest. Students who choose to explore future careers have built computers from scratch, designed and sewn clothing, engineered wind turbines, rehabilitated abused horses, or written "Beat" poetry. Others pursue potential lifelong hobbies: They learned to play a guitar, prepare a fender for painting, produce and edit digital video.

While some seniors do the required minimum, the vast majority of students use their culminating-project time to explore something of interest. As a result, they grow as individuals in an area of their choosing. They explore areas of passion.

Whether it be a full-fledged unit or prompts or problems, teachers and school systems honor individuality when they create activities where students contemplate their future.

The Reflective Teacher

- How do I give students the opportunity to ponder their futures in my classroom?

CLOSING

In an effort to raise their level of academics, many school districts are turning to tightly scripted curriculum aligned to state and school-district standards to assure students a quality, common learning experience. Within the bounds of any established curriculum, though, teachers should seek every opportunity to individualize the learning opportunities for students.

Thomas Edison, Bill Gates, Rachel Carson, and Rosa Parks didn't change the world because they wanted to be like the mainstream; they became great because they found their alternative path and followed it. Teachers should encourage students to find their own paths in life. They should also create activities and assessment methods that honor students' individuality.

Closing

Certainly, teaching can be segregated into its various steps. It can be dissected into its numerous duties. And when it is, the process can appear very complex and daunting, especially to the newcomer. Broken down into a series of techniques and strategies (as opposed to principles), teaching can become very logical and scientific and understandable, just like Van Gogh's *Starry Night* could, through analysis and dissection, be reduced to paint-by-numbers artwork.

Anyone who completed a paint-by-numbers art project as a kid, though, knows that you can create art by dabbing colors where the instructions ask—but something is still missing. When reducing great art to its parts then replicating it with appropriate shades and shadows, one gets a reproduction—yet some essence is lacking, something that defines the original artwork's greatness.

To some degree, teaching today suffers from this paint-by-numbers mentality. If teachers employ just the right series of techniques and strategies, the thinking goes, then students will learn. Teaching becomes mechanical.

Excellent teaching's sum, though, is much greater than all its strategies and techniques combined. Certainly there is a science to teaching, but there is also an art to this craft that creates a magic that borders on alchemy. Analysis of its technical parts does not explain what finally makes excellent teaching great. Nonquantifiable, human elements found in exceptional teachers do.

At its heart, great teaching is about passion. Outstanding educators love their content so deeply it becomes infectious—students are drawn in by a gravity of emotion that is irresistible. These classrooms are filled with an energy that tightly weaves various strategies and techniques. While what is taught in that classroom may fade with time, the students' memories of the teachers' love of their subject matter does not. Students come to enjoy a subject area because of a teacher's passion for it.

Great teaching is an act of faith. Exemplary teachers labor to design understanding that will prepare students for a world that will outlive the educators themselves. These teachers create understanding in the belief that it will, now or in the future, prove vital to students. Likewise, kind words, comments of confidence, and acts of assistance are given generously because they have the power to redirect lives. These exceptional teachers believe that in some great or small way their work as professionals will change the world for the better.

Great teaching is also about compassion. Outstanding educators care deeply for their students as people first. They know that with enough care and nurturing even the most reluctant students will turn their way. Content is important—but it is not foremost. These teachers steady the struggling and lift the downtrodden. They are flexible with rigid deadlines if the circumstances dictate. They celebrate individuality and uniqueness. These teachers know that the goal of education is to create complex, fully functioning adults—self-actualized beings, confident and prepared to reach for their dreams.

Finally, great teaching is also about confidence. Excellent teachers are confident in their abilities to connect with students. They believe their practice can lift the most needy learner. Under their guidance, they are confident that all kids can learn.

The Six Principles described in this book will in fact transform teaching practice, but they are incomplete without passion, faith, compassion, and confidence. When combined, the Six Principles and these human qualities create a chemistry of sorts, transforming what could be ordinary classrooms into positive, productive learning environments.

Notes

Principle 1: Make Kids Think

1. Richard W. Strong, Harvey F. Silver, and Matthew J. Perini, *Teaching What Matters Most: Standards and Strategies for Raising Student Achievement* (Alexandria, VA: Association for Supervision and Curriculum Development, 2001), 6–7.

2. Henry David Thoreau, "On the Duty of Civil Disobedience," n.d., at www.constitution.org/civ/civildis.htm (accessed Nov. 27, 2010).

3. Kate Di Camillo, *Because of Winn-Dixie* (Cambridge, MA: Candlewick Press, 2000).

4. Elie Wiesel, *Night* (New York: Hill & Wang, 2006).

Principle 2: Teach Big Ideas

1. Grant Wiggins and Jay McTighe, *Understanding by Design*, exp. 2nd ed. (Alexandria, VA: Association for Supervision and Curriculum Development, 2005), 105–107.

2. John D. Bransford, Ann L. Brown, and Rodney R. Cocking, eds., *How People Learn: Brain, Mind, Experience, and School*, exp. ed. (Washington, DC: National Academy Press, 2002), 16.

3. "Washington State Office of Superintendent of Public Instruction," n.d., at k12.wa.us/ (accessed Nov. 10, 2010).

4. Harper Lee, *To Kill a Mockingbird* (New York: Warner Books, 1982).

5. Washington State Office of Superintendent.

6. "College Board AP European History," 2010, at www.collegeboard.com (accessed Nov. 10, 2010).

Principle 3: Nurture Student Learning

1. "Washington State Office of Superintendent of Public Instruction," n.d., at k12.wa.us/ (accessed Nov. 10, 2010).
2. RubiStar, n.d., at http://rubistar.4teachers.org/ (accessed Nov. 10, 2010).
3. Richard J. Stiggins, Judith A. Arter, Jan Chappuis, and Stephen Chappuis, *Classroom Assessment for Student Learning: Doing It Right—Using It Well* (Portland, OR: Educational Testing Service, 2007), 29–38.
4. Stephen R. Covey, *The Seven Habits of Highly Effective People*, First Fireside ed. (New York: Simon & Schuster, 1990), 150–156.
5. Stiggins et al., *Classroom Assessment*, 154
6. Stiggins et al., *Classroom Assessment*, 283.

Principle 4: Construct Meaning

1. Madeline Hunter, *Enhancing Teaching* (New York: Macmillan College Publishing, 1994), 95.
2. Sandra Cisneros, *The House on Mango Street* (New York: Vintage Contemporaries, 1991).
3. Robert J. Marzano, *Building Background Knowledge for Academic Achievement* (Alexandria, VA: Association for Supervision and Curriculum Development, 2004), 3.
4. Marzano, *Building Background Knowledge*, 14.
5. Harper Lee, *To Kill a Mockingbird* (New York: Warner Books, 1982).
6. Marzano, *Building Background Knowledge*, 35–40.
7. *Springboard Level 4* (Princeton, NJ: College Board, 2011).
8. Richard J. Stiggins, Judith A. Arter, Jan Chappuis, and Stephen Chappuis, *Classroom Assessment for Student Learning: Doing It Right—Using It Well* (Portland, OR: Educational Testing Service, 2007), 225–229.
9. Grant Wiggins and Jay McTighe, *Understanding by Design*, exp. 2nd ed. (Alexandria, VA: Association for Supervision and Curriculum Development, 2005), 157–160.

Principle 5: Build Relationships

1. "Stress: Portrait of a Killer," DVD, produced by Stanford University and National Geographic Television (National Geographic Society, 2008).

Principle 6: Honor Individuality

1. Carol Ann Tomlinson and Jay McTighe, *Integrating Differentiated Instruction and Understanding by Design* (Alexandria, VA: Association for Supervision and Curriculum Development, 2006), 133.

Index